101

QUESTIONS AND ANSWERS FOR MANAGING AN ACCOUNTING PRACTICE

BY EDWARD MENDLOWITZ, CPA

Real-World, Time-Tested Solutions
for the Most Difficult Problems
Practitioners Face Every Day

*With tables, checklists, sample letters,
illustrative examples, real-life stories,
and step-by-step instructions*

Published by CPA Trendlines / Bay Street Group LLC, P.O. Box. 5139, East Hampton, N.Y. 11937 USA. baystreetgroup.com / 1 (631) 604-1651 / cpatrendlines.com

ISBN-13: 9780991266227
ISBN-10: 0991266226

Dedication

This book is dedicated to Norman Lipshie

With sadness I learned that Norman Lipshie passed away while this book was going through its final editing.

Norman was one of the main reasons I reach out to help fellow professionals. Over 35 years ago Norman, whom I did not know at that time, heard I was working on an extremely complicated financial transaction and he called me expressing concern that if I did not know how to handle it fully, he would like to give me some insights. Well, it turns out that until speaking to him I did not realize that I was in way over my head and he helped me immensely so that I was not embarrassed.

His call was gracious and unsolicited and came out of the blue. Norman's action became a role model for me and I resolved to do likewise if the situation came up. Every time I am asked to help a fellow professional I think fondly of Norman and willingly do what I can to assist them. This book is a product of some of my payback.

Norman was a true gentleman and a proud credit to our profession.

Norman, you were a great man. Rest in Peace my friend.

– Ed Mendlowitz

Foreword

I first met Ed Mendlowitz at a local chamber of commerce networking event, where we were doing our usual thing of shaking hands and meeting new people. That brief happenstance introduction, however, proved to be the beginning of a mutually rewarding relationship between Ed, myself and the successful firm we share in today.

Soon after that chamber event, a lunch meeting was arranged between me, Ed and his two other partners at the time, Peter Weitsen and Frank Boutillette. We spent over two-and-a-half hours chatting about the accounting profession and the best way to run a practice, finding many things in common in terms of networking, new business philosophies, the high priority of great client service and how to attract, train and retain good staff. The lunch ultimately led to the merger of our firms in 2005. Nine years later, I can say that I got more than I gave.

Ed's mentorship of our partners and staff has been invaluable. His philosophies on managing an accounting firm, our clients and oneself are timeless, full of common sense and most importantly, successful.

Fred Withum, co-founder of our firm and one of my personal mentors, once told me there are hundreds of business books out there, and tens of thousands of competitors who read these books. The only people who are successful, however, are the ones with the discipline to follow through. Clearly, Ed possesses such discipline.

This book brings together Ed's forty-plus years of experience as an entrepreneur and a professional services provider. Its easy-to-ready Q&A format makes it a great reference tool for accountants at all stages of their career. My favorite chapter is the "Family Tree of Referrals," discussing how to work smarter by understanding the power of referral sources, and having the confidence that new business will come when deciding to cull unprofitable and irritating clients. It's sage advice which every partner at every CPA firm should follow.

Enjoy the book, and may you have the discipline to follow through on Ed's recommendations. You'll be a better person – and professional - for it.

– Bill Hagaman, Managing Partner & CEO
WithumSmith+Brown, PC

Introduction

For over 40 years I have asked fellow professionals for assistance, and for almost as long I have reached out to offer assistance. As professionals, we do not live and work in a vacuum. We need each other and the more we collaborate the more we all grow.

I have not done everything I would have liked to do, but through interaction with fellow CPAs, colleagues, other professionals, staff and clients I have learned many things and I've tried to refine some of those lessons here. Without sharing, I would not have been as successful. I have also learned that sharing causes me to grow also. It forces me to be clearer about what I do, be able to express myself better, help me better articulate my thoughts, and puts me in contact with some of the brightest people I know – my fellow CPAs.

At some point I realized that many of the questions repeated themselves and that most of us have the same concerns. For that reason I started to write up the most often asked questions with my answers. There are, of course, very few perfect answers. But, hopefully, through the thorough consideration of the question and the possible solutions, the best (if not perfect) answer can emerge. I hope that you can get some your questions answered here.

I welcome calls and emails with questions and I do my best to respond quickly. The more calls the better for all of us. The Q&As are posted weekly by CPA Trendlines at cpatrendlines.com and each month on the New Jersey Society of CPAs Open Forum. I also email them in bulk to those who request it. Send me your email and I'll add you to my mailing list. I hope you enjoy this book and don't hesitate to contact me: by phone: 1 (732) 964-9329 or by email: emendlowitz@withum.com.

– Ed Mendlowitz

Partners' Network

The Q&A is a response to questions asked by members of the WithumSmith+Brown, PC Partners' Network.

The WS+B Partners' Network is a program of WithumSmith+Brown, PC that is designed to support smaller practices by making available resources of our larger firm. It helps to broaden smaller firms' services and expertise; helps them build their business for growth and profitability; provides specialists to help with challenging audit and tax matters with a phone call; and to offer ideas and tips on how to better manage smaller accounting practices.

Benefits and membership information are available by contacting Ed, or Heather Suddoth at 1 (732) 828-1614 or hsuddoth@withum. com. Information is also in every issue of the Partners' Network Newsletter, at withum. com/serv_partnersnetwork_news. shtml

x

Acknowledgements

This book is based on thousands of calls I've gotten from fellow professionals over a long career. The Q&As attempt to condense them into an easy-to-read format. Thanks must go to everyone that has asked me questions, and I am indebted to all of them. Unfortunately I cannot recall all their names and if I did, space would likely not permit listing the names. But you know who you are and keep the calls coming.

This book is also the result of long-term collaboration with clients, partners and staff. Some that clearly and continuously come to mind are my partners Peter A. Weitsen, Frank R. Boutillette, William Hagaman, Jr. , John Mortenson, Ron Bleich, Ruben Cardona, Howard Stein and Shree Nadkarni.

Thanks to Rick Telberg for editing and publishing this book in the hope that it will extend the range of fellow professionals that can possibly benefit from these Q&A.

Everything I do, including this book, is done with the needed support and love of my wife Ronnie.

About the Author

Ed Mendlowitz is a partner in the New Brunswick, N. J., office of Withum Smith + Brown, PC, and has more than 40 years of public accounting experience. He is a licensed certified public accountant in the states of New Jersey and New York and is accredited by the American Institute of Certified Public Accountants (AICPA) in business valuation (ABV), certified in financial forensics (CFF) and as a personal financial specialist (PFS). He also has the AICPA CITP and CGMA designations. Ed is also admitted to practice before the United States Tax Court and has testified as an expert witness in federal and state court regarding business valuations.

A graduate of City College of New York, Ed earned his bachelor of business administration degree. He is a member of the AICPA, the New Jersey Society of Certified Public Accountants (NJSCPA) and the New York State Society of Certified Public Accountants (NYSSCPA). In addition, Ed was a founding partner of Mendlowitz Weitsen, LLP, CPAs, which merged with WS+B in 2005. Currently, he serves on the NYSSCPA Estate Planning Committee, and was chairman of the committee that planned the NYSSCPA's 100th anniversary. The author of over 20 books, Ed has also written hundreds of articles for business and professional journals and newsletters. He is a contributing editor to the *Practitioners Publishing Company's 1998/1999 706/709 Deskbook*, and current editions of *Wiley's Handbook on Budgeting, Corporate Controller's Handbook* and the *AICPA Management of an Accounting Practice Handbook* and is on the editorial board of *Bottom Line/Personal* newsletter. Appearing regularly on television news programs, Ed has also been quoted in many major newspapers and periodicals in the United States.

He is the recipient of the Lawler Award for the best article published during 2001 in the *Journal of Accountancy*.

Ed is a frequent speaker to many professional and business groups, including the AICPA, NJSCPA, NYSSCPA, American Management Association, the National Committee for Monetary Reform, University of Medicine and Dentistry in N. J. and many more. For 11 years, he taught courses on financial analysis, corporate financial policy and theory, monetary and fiscal policy and financial and managerial accounting in the MBA program at Fairleigh Dickinson University.

Ed posts updates twice a week to his blog at partners-network. com and is a featured commentator at cpatrendlines. com. CPA Trendlines provides actionable intelligence to tax, accounting and finance professionals.

CONTENTS

1. ■ 10 Reasons Clients Don't Pay, and What to Do about It

Q:

I always have large amounts owed to me from clients. Is there anything I can do about this?

A:

Absolutely! My feelings are that large A/R balances are your fault. Accounting fees are almost never material to a business' cost structure, but letting fees pile up can make them somewhat material.

We need to recognize that we are businesspeople and part of that is to maintain cash flow. I also find that one of the worst things about accounting is collecting what was billed. This is a usual question I get and usually get it when the accountant is frustrated because he or she needs to collect the money and gets a lot of heartache speaking to clients about the payment.

Based on many conversations I had with CPAs (and my own conversations with clients), here is a listing of some of the reasons clients give for not paying.

1. I misplaced the bill

2. I did not understand the bill

3. I thought I could pay it over time

4. I did not think it would be so high

5. I did not realize it was past due

6. I never pay a bill until I am asked to pay it three times

7. My bookkeeper should have paid it. Let me check with her

8. Business is slow and my customers haven't paid

9. I am waiting for a big check from a customer and when I get it, you will be the first person I'll pay

10. You made the bill out to the wrong company. As soon as you send me a correct bill, I'll pay it

One thing that truly upsets me is when clients ignore the bill and wait until they are badgered for payment. I detest doing that and resent that I haven't been promptly paid when I did the work promptly. I also get the feeling that if my call wasn't made, I would never be paid. Who do these people think they are? They are stealing from me! And, they resent my calls?!

When you neglect to ask for payment after sending the bill, and let it lie, you are either signalling that you think the bill was too high and don't really expect to be paid, or indicating that you are not a good businessperson. Either way, you will lose out.

I have a simple solution that has always worked for me. When I prepare my monthly bills and statements, I call anyone who did not pay the previous bill. I make the call myself – delegating this never seemed to work well for me. I tell the client that I noticed that the last bill wasn't paid and ask if there is a problem with the bill. If there is a problem, I can address it right then and there. If there is no problem, I tell them I would appreciate it if they could put a check in the mail right now, or give me a credit card to charge the payment.

Doing this is uncomfortable for sure, but it brings in the money and after a couple of such calls the client gets the idea they need to pay the bills timely. My hobby is collecting stamps, not working for people without being paid! This also limits my A/R build-up and reduces the really uncomfortable calls when large balances are past due.

2. Preparing to Sell Your Practice in a Few Years

Q:

I am getting older and want to continue working at least five more years. Should I merge now to anticipate and facilitate a buyout?

A:

Selling means retiring. Is that something you want to do? I've written many times about being clear about your goals and what you really want. That being said, here is a general discussion about the reality of the value of your practice.

13 Things You Need to Know Today

1. When we sell our practices, we will be taxed at near the highest rates we will probably ever be in, making our yield much less than what we were making. Because of this, many accountants hold on until just after the last minute — when it becomes our heirs' problem.

2. We are in a service business with no tangible product. Our reputation is our major asset. One large lawsuit can put us out of business, e. g. Arthur Andersen and Laventhol & Horwath. So can a series of large client losses, e. g. Oppenheim Appel & Dixon; and Clarence Raines. So can a serious illness such as a stroke or heart disease, or a tragic car accident. Also, a debilitating illness of a spouse can slow us up. I used examples of large firms that were well documented in the newspapers; however, there are many smaller firms that had the same unfortunate fates. Our sister profession – law – recently had a major bankruptcy – Dewey Leboeuf. Another high-profile legal bankruptcy was former baseball commissioner Bowie Kuhn's firm, Finley Kumble Wagner Underberg Manley Myerson & Casey. Values are illusory until payment is received in full.

3. And we get old. We may not feel old, and may have more energy than those half our age, but the perception of younger clients is that we are not for them. The longer you live, the longer your practice's value will dwindle. In general, clients want accountants who are contemporaries, or slightly older – not a generation older.

4. The asset value of the practice looks good on a personal financial statement, but only the cash flow from the sale will have any meaning to you. Even those amounts have shrunk – from 1½ to 2 times gross to 1 (or less) times gross. Many CPAs do not have a basic understanding of what a buyer would want and why they buy and do not position their practice for sale properly.

5. Many professionals assume they will retire some day in some way. Whether or not it is recognized and a timetable vaguely established, there is a value to the practice. If retirement is contemplated, then maximizing the value needs to be considered, and that also needs proper timing.

6. One way of quantifying that value is to consider what someone would pay for it and under what terms if you suddenly decided to leave it completely.

7. Add a transition period that you might want to remain for, and at what compensation.

8. Now, consider that it is not today when you are leaving, but sometime in the future, and that you will realize the practice's value at that time. What amount will that be?

9. Unless you then become like Merlin (who lived backwards), the practice would probably be less valuable at that time to an acquirer.

10. Measure the differences and add the excess of your earnings while you continue with the practice over what you would have earned on the net proceeds if you sold your practice.

11. How are you richer? That is your optimum financial alternative.

12. Keep in mind that buyers mainly want predictability of cash flow, and secondarily a "ticket" into business.

13. You should have a practice continuation agreement in event of an untimely death or disability.

3. ■ Why Selling Your Practice Is Not a Retirement Strategy

Q:

I've heard you say that you shouldn't count on anything from your practice when you decide to retire. Are you serious?

A:

I probably said that, but it was in the context of planning for guaranteed cash flow in retirement. A practice's value is never guaranteed until the checks clear.

I did say that it is important to create an asset base for retirement and that this can come from a number of sources – and we each need to assign an importance to each source and a probability of its providing a comfortable retirement.

Here are what I see as the probable sources:

1. Social Security
2. Tax-sheltered/deferred savings (pensions, IRAs, annuities and

possibly cash-value life insurance) policies

3. Savings and investments not in tax-deferred accounts. This includes liquid and non-liquid assets

4. Proceeds from sale of your practice or retirement buyout

5. Sale of your residence

6. Your children or other family members

Which of the above are guaranteed?

Social Security will be guaranteed, but won't be enough for most of our retirements. Tax-sheltered savings as well as liquid assets in non-tax-deferred accounts are guaranteed and will provide a source of cash flow unless you invest foolishly. Illiquid assets shouldn't be counted on. Selling your practice is not a guaranteed way and will be subject to many factors including the ability of the buyer to make all the payments. Also, your cash flow will only be the after-tax return on the investment of the net proceeds. Selling a residence is baloney – you will always need to live somewhere and nursing homes and senior residences are pretty expensive. An alternative is taking perpetual cruises – in inside rooms – figure it out – much cheaper and possibly better treatment since you are their customer. Your children – Ha Ha. You might be lucky if you don't have to support them.

My "guaranteed" solution: Maximize your annual contributions to tax-sheltered accounts and try to save something extra in your own names. Invest wisely and don't be stupid!

4. 10 Questions to Ask Yourself Before You Decide to Add Financial Services to Your Practice

Q:

I am thinking of adding financial services to my practice. What are your thoughts?

A:

For starters, "financial services" means selling investment products or managing money. This is different from adding financial planning, which I see as an extension of and a next step to sound tax planning for clients.

Getting into the financial services business requires tremendous effort, training, licenses and a long startup period until a critical mass can be attained where there will be a reasonable cash flow and profit. This business involves the ability to sell and then deliver. Many large organizations thought that CPA practices could be fertile ground for additional business and companies such as American Express and H&R Block acquired CPA practices to get access to the tax clients who would need "product" or investment management. I only know what I read in the newspapers, but they seemed to be glad to get out of this business because they sold the practices they bought at big losses. I can only assume the model did not work – accountants weren't able to sell these products and services. I also get many calls – as many from financial planners in brokerage and insurance firms inquiring about opportunities to work in CPA firms. Some of them, after working a dozen or more years, weren't earning reasonable incomes for their stage of life and they know they would have done better had they started out in, or not left, public accounting, and now want to get back in.

Many accountants ask me this because they believe they can make more money. My first bit of advice if they want to make more money is to try to do more of what they are already doing in their current practices.

However, not to beat a dead horse – here are some specifics to consider.

1. Prepare a business plan and consider:

    a. How much revenue will be received during the first 36 months and whether you can make profit on it
    b. Where clients will come from, how many and revenue per client
    c. How you will deliver the services – will it be done internally with existing resources or outsourced?
    d. Which partner will be in charge and will oversee the new business
    e. Who on your staff will be able to perform these services
    f. If an investment is needed how much and how will it be funded

2. What will happen to your existing practice, or the part of the practice the partners and staff moving over to the financial services had been performing?

3. Do you have the expertise internally?

4. What licenses and credentials are needed, what type of entity will be formed or will it be part of your present practice, and what type of liability insurance will be needed? Whether you know it or not, you are starting a new business.

5. Try to imagine how you will feel and respond to clients if you are managing money and the market takes a freefall such as it did in the end of 2008 and beginning of 2009.

6. Find products that you think clients most likely would need and find out your commission structure and whether clients would buy them in adequate volume.

7. If you are to offer true financial planning along with the sale of products, will you have a wide enough knowledge of competing and alternative products so that your clients won't be pigeonholed into one provider's merchandise?

8. Many financial services clients expect financial planning and possibly tax preparation as part of the overall service, at no additional fees. If this is so, you might lose revenue you are currently receiving.

9. If you are so interested in this area, have you attended a reasonable number of conferences and CPE programs so you have an adequate exposure to the arena, or will this be a new "just got the idea" type of venture for you?

10. You should compare this new venture with using the same effort to expand services you are presently offering your clients.

Good luck!

5. Should I Really Spend the Time Using Checklists?

Q:

I know you preach using checklists, but are they really necessary? I don't like using them.

A:

Yes – you should use checklists. I use checklists for everything I do – including packing for a trip or vacation. If you want to go further, a great book about checklists is *The Checklist Manifesto: How to Get Things Right* by Atul Gawande.

P. S. : The CPA who asked me this question has called me a few times over the years when he had serious problems both in poorly prepared tax returns with insufficient backup and negligently prepared financial statements. I helped him considerably and he got out of situations (barely) that caused him many sleepless nights. I always pointed out that if he used such and such checklist, he most likely would have avoided the problems he had and, in my opinion, created. Now he asks me if they are "really that necessary"?

6. ■ Are Partner Retreats Really Worth the Cost?

Q:

Is there any value to a retreat?

A:

Absolutely! Retreats are very important to reconnect with your partners and reassert why you are in business and what you hope to accomplish, in addition to making a living and not having to work for a boss who isn't as good or nice as you are.

I had retreats with my partners in various forms. We went to out-of-town hotels; had full-day off-site meetings; spent a day strolling on a college campus; and traveled to AICPA conferences in Las Vegas, Disney World, New Orleans and similar fun places.

Variously, we prepared agendas in advance, "negotiated" agendas before we started or discussed ideas as they seemed to arise. One time Peter and I spent three hours in a parked car in a shopping center where I went to buy some new magic tricks after leaving the Hard Rock Café in Orlando and we formulated the ideas that became the Partners' Network. Another time we spent a day walking from the tip of Manhattan up to Madison Square Garden, stopping along the way to pop in at clients' offices, and came up with the QuickBooks® consulting service that has provided us with more than a few hundred thousand dollars of business. And one time after spending a day in a local hotel room, Peter, Frank and I came up with some ideas that increased realization 5% directly adding to our bottom line. Going back to the early 1980s, my partners, Sy Siegel and Paul Rich, and I, and our key managers came up with a method of exciting our staff that increased productivity and decreased turnover.

Retreats work and I highly recommend them.

Partners' retreats are an excellent way to take some time to reflect, plan, strategize, and assess your practice. Actually, it should be more appropriately called a partners' advance!

7. ■ Audit Reports Without Doing the Work?

Q:

I have a friend who runs a small CPA firm. He has a client who owns some motels across the U. S. who sold them to a large company.

Their auditor, a Big 4 firm, would like to review his prior year audit papers and he has asked me to review his work papers beforehand and make sure that they are in good shape for the Big 4 firm. As he is a small practice, his work papers are likely to be not as sophisticated as the Big 4 is used to seeing.

Do you know to what extent he would be required to show his work? Would it be sufficient to show the trial balance with a narrative indicating the work performed on each line item that is deemed to be in scope? Would it be sufficient to show a checklist indicating the procedures performed? Would he be required to show all the detailed work papers?

A:

If he performed an audit and followed proper procedures including being peer reviewed, then his work papers should be in order and not need any oversight by you.

Based upon our conversation it seems this CPA did not do the minimum work required for an audit, did not use applicable checklists and audit programs, was not peer reviewed and is in serious violation of state licensing requirements. If he is an AICPA member, he also is in breach of their requirements. It also is clear to me that you are not competent to review his work. I suggest you pass on this. He has a problem that he does not understand.

I am glad I don't know who he is, and that he didn't call me. If he did, I would certainly talk to him. I am posting this as a precaution to other small practitioners that issue "audit" reports where they do not do the prescribed work. You need to do what needs to be done!

8. ■ Asking An Attorney for a Referral Fee

Q:

I referred a large amount of business to an attorney friend and she hasn't reciprocated. I asked her for a referral fee and she declined. I'd like to keep referring her because she does a great job for my clients and that makes me look good too. What should I do?

A:

It is always the right thing to look out for your clients' best interests. Referring the best attorney you know for a job is the right thing to do. However, you are in business and need to nurture referral sources. Attorneys are major referral sources and relationships should be "managed" to get the best work for clients while keeping the door open for reciprocal referrals from them. Referral sources are one form of your business currency and should be spent appropriately. I believe you should always refer the best person to your clients, but where that best person is not reciprocating, you should actively look for alternative people to refer. This requires you to develop new relationships, and find out their areas of expertise and responsiveness to clients' demands.

You should not have asked for a referral fee, which is unethical for the attorney to pay. If the attorney had given you something, I would question her repute and probably would not refer her going forward.

Follow-up: This question dealt with referrals to an attorney that were not reciprocated.

Here is my short list of "business currency":

1. Your contacts
2. Your clients
3. What you know
4. Your interest in what you do
5. Internal pride in your work
6. The ability to apply everything together every time it is necessary

I've identified six items that represent "currency. " Currency is what you use to get new business and develop and grow your practice. Don't pass up an opportunity to increase your currency account. Look for ways to refer other professionals, maintain and nurture relationships, certainly keep track of whom you know and let them hear from you on a regular basis.

More than 30 years ago, one of my friends — a managing partner of a reasonably sized firm — had a growth plan. Part of it required every partner to have contact with clients at least once every three months – and had them report that contact.

Seems micro, but it was one of the reasons the firm grew to become one of the top 15 firms in the nation. Clients are who pay our salary and who recommend additional clients. Keeping in touch is a must. Yet I know many CPAs who do not have much interest in regularly keeping in touch, and they are the most surprised when they lose a client.

Duh! I just realized that I did not include "Reputation" on that list. Perhaps it should be there. Is there anything else that can be included? What would you put on your currency list?

9. What You Need to Know Before Expanding Into Business Valuation

Q:

I am exploring the business valuation credential as a way to expand our practice. I'm still (relatively) young to the profession and would (I think) love to expand into this niche area.

A few things:

> 1) We don't do any BV now so my ability to acquire the ABV credential would be difficult without the experience aspect.

> 2) Do you have any knowledge of or experience with the ABV Credential Experience Program facilitated by the AICPA?

> 3) If I don't go that route, any thought to getting a "lesser" credential that doesn't require the experience and then "upgrade" to the ABV once I get a few engagements under my belt?

A:

I wouldn't try to talk anyone out of getting into business valuation services, but I would point out the difficulties of entering the field, and what you need to do to succeed in it.

There are quite a few credentials in the BV field, and they all require study, knowledge and experience. Studying you can do yourself. Knowledge comes with understanding and applying what you study. Experience comes with doing the work for varied clients and situations. The credential is evidence of your expertise, but is not conclusive. The extent of your expertise is how well you do your work and can document and support what you've done in a credible manner.

I have the AICPA ABV and CFF credentials. You can pursue these by getting info from the AICPA or any of the other designations by contacting the certifying organization.

Many engagements call for valuations where you do not issue written reports similar in size to a small book. For example, "valuations" are done when you have discussions with clients regarding selling their business, buying a business, valuing the business in their personal financial statement or on a loan application, how their assets would be divided in a divorce or should be valued in a buy-sell agreement, or how they can transfer some ownership to a child working in the business. All of these situations are "experience. " The quality of experience could vary from very low to very high depending on the involvement of the work you do to obtain the valuation amounts you suggest to them.

I recommend attending full-day state society business valuation conferences and their BV committee meetings. After you get a good taste of the area, I recommend the AICPA annual three-day business valuation conference. Many webinars also offer excellent instruction.

The best way to get experience and to learn is to work on BV engagements with those who are more experienced. If you work for a firm that does these, ask to work on such assignments. If you work for a firm that doesn't do them, perhaps consider getting a job with a firm that does, although if you are not absolutely sure you want to do this, you might be chasing your tail. If you have your own practice and neither you nor your partners have this experience, then study and attend conferences and webinars.

Great reference sources are

- *Understanding Business Valuation*, Third Edition, by Gary R. Trugman and
- *Divorce: The Accountant as Financial Expert* by Kalman A. Barson, both published by the AICPA.

Great newsletters are

- *BVR Business Valuation Update* by www. bvresources. com,
- *Financial Valuation and Litigation Expert* published by www. valuationproducts. com and
- Leimberg's e-newsletters published by leimbergservices. com.

There are other books and newsletters, but any of these is a good start.

BV is a very technical area that frequently needs you to defend your work. You have to know what you are doing, and that takes continuous updating. You need to be committed to this, and there are no shortcuts.

As a follow-up, here are…

47 Types of Business Valuation Services

1. Business valuation

2. Valuation for a succession plan

3. Valuation for an estate or gift

4. Will dispute

5. Estate alleging misconduct by a professional (attorney or accountant)

6. Valuation for "buy-sell" agreement

7. Settling "buy-sell" conflicts

8. Business split-up (valuation and forensic accounting)

9. Conflicts between brothers and sisters, parent and child, or divorced spouses still working in the same business

10. Allocating purchase price for book and tax purpose in a merger or sale or acquisition

11. Advising a creditor's committee in a bankruptcy

12. Looking for assets and asset tracing

13. Analyzing future cash flow and profitability

14. Matrimonial disputes

15. Matrimonial – settling post-judgment disputes

16. Tracing of flow of funds

17. Determining income and assisting in preparation of case information statement in a divorce

18. Lifestyle analysis

19. Determining value of premarital assets and/or retirement funds

20. Pre-filing consultation

21. Economic damages – lost wages, health insurance costs and lost retirement savings as a result of being forced to retire early

22. Industry-specific knowledge

23. Income analysis

24. Joint marital tax returns

25. Child support substantiation or verification

26. Post-judgment change of circumstances

27. Evaluating business interests

28. Calculating damages

29. Damages and loss from a fire

30. Special counsel investigation of contributions to qualified and non-qualified deferred compensation plans on behalf of an individual over a prolonged period

31. Business succession between parents and child, and between siblings and between children and key person running business where "promises" were made but never put in writing

32. Management fees allocated to costs in a cost-plus project

33. Professional malpractice charges – plaintiff or defense cases

34. Lost wages

35. Damages caused by a disability caused by a landlord

36. Verifying tax rates used on individual tax returns are correct

37. Determining tax rates to apply to assets that will be subject to, or partially subject to, income tax

38. Determining built-in gain for C corporation conversion to S status

39. Fair value for financial statement purposes

40. Deriving merger ratio between related parties

41. Stock split-up valuation

42. Economic reasonableness of a management agreement and adherence to it

43. Restructuring of revolving, working capital, equipment or mortgage debt

44. Structuring a management buyout

45. Valuing assets seized by government agency or as a result of a judgment

46. Lost royalties in a patent or copyright dispute

47. Damages from a construction delay

These engagements can arise from a party to the transaction, insurance company, mediator, arbitrator, attorney, another CPA, other professional, trustee, executor, administrator or court appointment. The engagements can be original work, critiques or rebuttals as an advocate, expert or consultant.

10. Clients' Calls at Home

Q:

I try to respond quickly to my clients' calls and emails but now they even call me at home. What can I do about this?

A:

You told me you have an office and also give your clients your cell number to use. You also told me that you carry a smartphone and told your clients you prefer emails and can respond quicker to them. You also told me you get many compliments on your responsiveness.

You also said that you return calls on your home phone at night and on clients' phones when you are at their offices. This can't be done. In the old days, this was common, but now caller ID engraves every phone number, making it easy just to redial that number by clicking it.

You have to stop returning calls on any phone other than your office or cell phone. If calls are made to your home phone, don't answer them and let your clients know the next time you speak to them that they should use your cell (or office) number as your main number and not any of the others, especially your home number. You need some down time and privacy and the home should be off limits.

What you can also do is tell clients to call your office during the day and cell after business hours, and return calls during those hours on the appropriate phone.

I have found that many people now send emails or make calls at all hours of the day or night as they think of something – and they make it your responsibility to get back to them. They do not expect immediate responses but it is their way to get it off their minds.

One of my pet peeves is serial call returners. These are people you play phone tag with and then give a specific time range when you can be reached and they respond as soon as they get your message even though it is not within that time range. I've gotten to the point where I no longer call them back – they were told when to reach me and chose to ignore it by calling me when they knew I was not available. It is inconsiderate and indicates a self-centered lack of respect or an abnormal compulsiveness – either way – not my problem!

11. Dealing With Busy Season Demands

Q:

It is tax season and I am working around the clock but sometimes I seem to be chasing my tail and not getting everything done I should. How can I deal with this?

A:

Tough question and very common issue. We all have these problems at times, and especially during tax season. We are all very busy then, but we are also always busy all year round. It is clear what we need to do with the bulk of the work – get it done. Instead of being overwhelmed with a "pile" or work, take 15 or 20 minutes each morning to prioritize what needs to be done that day. If it is not essential, then schedule it for post-tax season and get it off your mind right now. If it is one of those truly important items, but not urgent, I would put it near the top and get it done now.

I just did something like that last week. A very important client called with a question about something that was on his mind and he said he was hesitant to mention it now, and said I could call him with the response after tax season. I said I would but then I did it right away – it took me 25 minutes – and I called him with the answer later that day. He was truly impressed and grateful. And I got it off my mind.

I figure if it was important enough to him to call me, then I should help him by getting it off his mind!

However, most of the extras we possibly should do don't have the excruciating April 15 deadline, so we pass them forward.

If you are reading this during busy season, you recognize the value of practice management and should be commended. The work needs to get out. We know that effective delegation can push much of the detail or repetitive work down and permit you to do the thinking, planning, analysis and big picture look the clients expect from you and are willing to pay for. So adopt effective management as your personal culture.

Maybe you can't start now, and possibly shouldn't, but really look around and assess the type of work you are doing. If your billing rate is two or three times that of a staff person and you are doing staff-level work, then in reality you are only worth the salary of the lower-level person who should be doing the work. Make some notes of how the work can be delegated and in May start trying to implement a procedure so you won't have this problem next tax season.

12. Can You Teach Judgment?

Q:

Recently a colleague asked me, "How do you teach judgment?" and before I could respond, he answered it himself with "You can't teach judgment!"

A:

Everyone working for you has and uses judgment – they have homes, families, organizations they belong to and they manage their careers. Each of these requires their exercising judgment many times a day. They all have judgment.

What they might not have at work is experience and the empowerment to use their judgment – and that is usually their bosses' fault. It could be their fault if they want to be positioned to grow and they aren't given the opportunity and they don't reach out for that opportunity. Then they remain in that dead-end position without trying to better it. Putting that aside, it is their boss' fault for not seeing that they get the proper experience to be able to exercise reasonable judgment to get as much work as possible done at lower levels.

The boss, who is the one to complain about their direct report not exercising judgment, is the culprit. Their subordinate has not been given the opportunity of exposure to accumulate the experience to be able to make the right decisions most of the time, and where they have, they have not been empowered to make it – even if it is a wrong decision. The mistakes are where they will learn. They should not be put in the situation where a client can be lost, or a bank loan called, but mistakes come from exercising judgment, and so does growth and responsibility. Experience comes from the exposure and learning from mistakes.

P. S.: People learn and absorb relative to their exposure, their attention and awareness, role models, how they seek out learning and growth openings and their frames of reference. As a boss or supervisor, you need to manage each of these opportunities for growth.

13. What Do You Think You're Doing?

Q:

Sometimes I get stuck doing work that the client did not ask me to do, that is not chargeable and simply a waste of time, but I get trapped (by myself). Any words of wisdom to avoid this?

A:

Yes. Ask yourself this simple question:

• If the client knew what you were doing and the cost, would he or she pay for it?

Ask yourself this every time you find yourself chasing your tail or veering off course. I use a half-hour limit and define this as working on something for a half-hour without any progress.

Also set a time and cost budget before you start anything, and ask yourself whether the client would pay that fee for that work in that manner.

Also, let's say you have a partner; what would she say when you told her you couldn't bill for what you did?

This is called management. But effective management doesn't happen – it is not air, always there – it needs to be done consciously and deliberately. Management! Do it!

14. Measuring Growth in Yourself, Staff and Partners

Q:

I suspect that my partner has "maxed out" and cannot grow further, which will retard our growth. What can I do or how can I deal with this?

A:

This is a frequent question, and sometimes it is the person asking it who has "maxed out. " But, sometimes it is the partner or a key staff member who wants to be made a partner.

I developed a Knowledge Gap ("KG") method to provide a way of measuring the difference in growth when you interact with people. This includes those over you and under you from the same firm, and clients and other professionals and colleagues.

You would "measure" the difference when you first meet or started working with them. Over time if the KG narrows, the less knowledgeable is growing faster. If it widens the more knowledgeable person is growing faster.

If you are mentoring a new employee, the gap should narrow because of the faster rate he would be learning. When you work with a new client, and your knowledge of her business is lower than hers, the KG should narrow as you work with the client. If it widens giving an unfavorable KG, it would indicate your decreasing relevance or importance, or your lack of growth relative to the client.

This measure should be adjusted depending upon the type of interaction you have. For instance, the KG difference is highly relevant if you are functioning as a consultant or advisor to a client and passing on what you know so your clients adopt it. It might not have much importance if you are providing bookkeeping services to a business owner while she is looking to hire a full-time bookkeeper.

With regard to benefits from interactions with specific people, to the extent that they don't "teach" you anything, the KG would not narrow – and you lose out, and perhaps you need to examine the relationship. Another way to look at it is that a person's KG value would remain high if he is unable to teach or mentor others, which is really his own ineptitude. However, he probably won't be growing either and the KG should narrow because of your growth from other sources.

It is also possible and likely that there are many different situations where the KG could be measured with the same people. For example, an entry-level accountant would know much less than the person training her in auditing, but might know much more on how to handle data mining or sampling software – which she would have just learned in college.

Following are some questions that put the KG to use…

Using the Knowledge Gap Method

1. Measure the difference between the total sum of the pertinent knowledge between you and your client.

_____

_____

_____

2. Has that difference increased or decreased since you started as their accountant?

_____

_____

_____

3. Now measure the difference between you and your staff (individually).

_____

_____

_____

4. Has that difference increased or decreased since they came to work in your office?

_____

_____

_____

5. Now do the same with your partners (individually).

_____

_____

_____

6. Has that difference increased or decreased since you became partners?

_____

_____

_____   _____

Think about your answers.

Example

The following shows how I actually used the KG method to measure my interactions with Peter Weitsen after we became partners.

> *Initially I knew more than Peter in procedures dealing with the IRS. He had more knowledge in tax research and I had more knowledge in estate planning (but not much more). As our relationship and partnership grew, Peter's knowledge and skills in dealing with the IRS and tax research greatly surpassed mine with a very wide KG in his favor. At some point, I realized that, weaned myself away from those areas, and concentrated my skills in estate planning and greatly increased that KG. Being partners, it is not necessary, and is counterproductive, if we have the same strengths. Using the KG method enabled each of us to direct our efforts to becoming expert in different areas of the practice.*

> *At the time, the two areas Peter was extremely adept in were more important to our practice, while the estate planning was less so. Abdicating those two areas to him while not needing as much time in my area freed me up to find other specialties to concentrate on, such as valuations of the gifts made because of the estate planning, enabling our practice to grow further.*

The above mentions three specific areas. However, there were much more than these areas between us, and the KG approach provided a means to decide where each of us should focus our efforts.

P. S. : The response tells how to "measure" your suspicion. I did not address how to deal with a partner who is not growing. That is a difficult issue and requires an assessment of the total relationship including within and outside the firm. Part of the evaluation is their relationship with clients, and while they might have maxed out in professional skills, they might be the one maintaining the client relationships or bringing in new business. I recently heard a speaker say that if you are the smartest person in the room, you have a problem. Maxing out is a subjective term defined by one person in the relationship, and not necessarily reality. There are checklists and MAP programs that define roles of partners and these should be used or attended. Also, my ultimate test is whether you are making sufficient income. If so, why upset the applecart?

15. When Not to Offer a Free Initial Consultation

Q:

I was wondering what your thought is regarding initial consultation fees.

Currently, I do not charge a fee for an initial consultation, and it seems that most CPAs do not charge either (at least not the sole practitioners that I know). Would the fee deter new clients or actually weed out the ones who are most likely not going to become clients anyway? If a fee is charged, then how much, and how long should the consultation last? Should the fee be applied to any work that I am eventually engaged to do?

A:

There seems to be a toss-up between two different philosophies: people value something more when they pay for it, and you don't want to create any barriers to entry.

I always charge for an initial consultation *except* if the consultation is for a substantial business client or a big work project (such as preparing five years of tax returns or an FBAR situation). Most (over 65%) of my initial consultations provide the information the client is seeking and there is definite value to the meeting. If they don't want to pay, I see no reason to spend MY time, and pass on it.

Most of my initial consultations do not lead to additional business since they have their answers. Of the remaining, about a quarter lead to additional work, so I am paid for all of my meetings and about 8% result in additional work on bigger projects.

The types of initial consultations I have are:

- business valuation;

- estate planning;

- succession planning;

- tax planning;

- financial planning, business plan and projections; and

- leveraged or management buyouts.

Following is a draft of an initial consultation engagement letter that I have used.

While this deals with a valuation, it can be adapted to most any situation; and I have. I also quote a fixed fee that is somewhat based on the value of the meeting to the client. There is no need to quote an hourly rate on this type of situation that I am hoping will lead to additional services and many people do not relate kindly to hourly rates and open ended time possibilities.

Sample Initial Business Valuation Consultation Engagement Proposal

Dear Mr. Accountant,

You asked me what was involved in work, time and the cost of performing a valuation for a client of yours.

Based on what you told me, I do not believe your client would need a formal conclusion of value. Rather, he seems to need a discussion providing an indication of the value and a method that could accomplish what he wants. In most situations, I can cover that in an hour and half consultation. The fee for that would be $_____, including all of my advance preparation.

If your client needs the valuation for a tax-based transaction, transfer or estate tax return, he would need a conclusion of value for the fair market value prepared in accordance with IRS rulings and requirements. I could quote on that, but this does not seem to be the case here.

Note that the fee does not include any memos, calculations or written documentation. The client should not need it, but he could take all the notes he wants at the meeting. You as well as his attorney or other advisors could be at the meeting.

Once I need to put something in writing, it becomes very involved. I have to state the facts, issues, purposes of valuation, include an extensive discussion not only providing the methodology of my determination of value, but why alternative methods are not applicable, have to address or offer explanations of eight specific items the IRS wants to see covered and applied as applicable to the company being valued, apply adjustments and explain why, for control or minority interests, and discuss other potential issues that become a lengthy and costly process not necessarily adding to the determination of the value for your client's purposes. I also will have to include detailed calculations and to follow procedures under AICPA Standards for Valuation Services that will add quite a bit of time. Further, I will need to have the report proofread and reviewed internally, adding more time.

My method of getting the information, reviewing it, running some numbers that I could refer to at the meeting and preparing a presentation tailored to the client's situation, with the ramifications explained, seems to work well and is cost-effective for the client. It is also done at a fixed fee regardless of the time I need to spend once I get the requested information.

Note that I am accredited by the AICPA in Business Valuation, Financial Forensics, Personal Financial Planning and am the author of a book on succession planning that was published by the AICPA, as well as dozens of speeches and articles on business valuation and succession planning.

In case the client wants to proceed, I attached a document request. I would need as much of that information as possible as well as a check payable to my firm or credit card authorization for $_____.

If any questions, do not hesitate to call me (cell: _____).

16. Why No One Listens to You

Q:

I notice that most of the time my staff doesn't listen when I talk. How can I make them listen?

A:

Err, what did you say? Just kidding! I find this issue very widespread. I believe there is an epidemic of people not listening, not just staff.

Clients, partners, colleagues, associates, fellow professionals, and vendors are all guilty of not listening. I notice this almost daily, and it is tedious and extremely annoying. People call me with questions and only hear what they want to hear, which is usually very little. Others don't listen because they perceive themselves as "being too important to spend time listening. " Some clients are not happy with their lives so no answer can satisfy them.

In some respect people live in their own world with them being the nucleus and everyone else orbiting planets. It is almost like a parallel existence.

We all seem continuously distracted, with a lack of focus and inattention. A real epidemic!

What to do about it? Be clear about what you say and say as little as you can to get your point across. Keep things simple and don't make multiple statements or requests. Don't get into long diatribes. I think you are better dealing with more brief calls or conversations than one long one. This creates more interruptions, but I believe it is more effective.

Also, when all else fails, don't put yourself in a position of having to deal with these boors unless you have absolutely no choice. Life is too short!

Oh, and don't you become one of them!

P. S. Just after I wrote this, I had to drive somewhere and my wife started giving me directions and I typically did not pay attention to her. I thought of what I just wrote, and asked her to repeat it and I really listened to her the second time. Result: I got to where I was going without a hitch and without having to take the GPS out of my glove compartment and start programming in where I needed to be. It works!

17. ■ How to Do It All?

Q:

My boss asked me to call you.

I am a staff accountant with five years experience. I am having a lot of stress trying to manage everything I have to do. I am juggling supervising people I don't know how to supervise, being managed less by those above me and having to figure out more for myself – including things I never did before or in industries I never worked on previously, keeping current with changes in accounting rules and taxes (since I am more like a generalist and clients ask me everything), never seeming to have any free time, juggling my schedule because most of my clients are never ready when they say they will be and being accountable to my boss for everything I do plus what the staff working under me does.

So how do I do it all? How can I prioritize all my responsibilities?

A:

Wow! Deep question! It seems there is very little written for "entry-level" supervisors, but plenty for people already doing it. There are no "how-to's" for this. Maybe this can be a start.

Here are some random thoughts, in no particular order…

15 Tips for the Novice Manager

1. First, you need to prioritize your responsibilities based on what is most important down to the least important.

2. The definition of importance should be based on how what you are doing, or need to do, measures up against your and the firm's big-picture goals.

3. You need to recognize that irrespective of your advanced position, you still need to take the time (and pester your boss if necessary) to make sure you fully understand what you need to do.

4. Try to identify training and supervision shortcomings of your bosses when you were just starting out and make sure you do not replicate them.

5. Ditto with great things they did and copy those too.

6. Clear instructions have to be your mantra – very clear. Never assume that your charge will understand what you mean. And you should make sure you are not assuming what your boss wants you to do. Keep in mind the famous Felix Unger quote, "When you assume, you make an 'ass' of 'u' and 'me. '"

7. Recognizing your inexperience in supervising staff is a mature move on your part, and you should be commended for that. Seeking help gets you another commendation. Speak to the managers and partners in your firm. Make your intrusions into 15-minute management tips. Cover one or two issues at a time. Be prepared when you speak to them and be specific. I don't think any manager or partner would think that a 15-minute break to help you is bothersome. Do it two or three times a week, not more. You don't want to be a pest, don't want to reach a point of diminishing returns and don't want to repeat yourself.

8. Keeping current is important and needs to be done. You can do this at home in the evening, or get to the office a little early and do it there.

9. At a five-year level, you should start to think about specializing. This can be in an industry such as manufacturing, real estate, contracting or not-for-profits, or specialty such as auditing, tax planning, forensic investigations or business valuations. Once a specialization is decided upon, you need to go about making yourself an expert – read, join professional associations, take focused CPE and try to write articles or give speeches. You need to do a lot of self-assessment when you decide on a specialty and you should enlist the help of the partners in your firm. Find out where they need a role filled, and have them commit to your proceeding in that area.

10. Clients not being ready and needing to change your schedule are unfortunately a common occurrence. You can mitigate the inconveniences caused by this by becoming more insistent and forceful about having available what you will need when you schedule the date. And never assume the client will do what they say. You'll need to follow up – follow up and then follow up. If there is the strong possibility they will not have what you need when you need it, speak to your immediate supervisor or manager. Let them contact their counterpart at the client to inform them about the compliance failure.

11. Despite your best efforts, your schedule will at times be overloaded and you will have multiple emergency priorities. Rather than taking on more than you can physically handle, let your boss prioritize the assignments (in coordination with other partners). It is their job to make the triage decisions. It is amazing how much pressure is removed when you go to them. I know that you don't want to say you can't do something, or that you are too busy to get something done. However, an initial reality-check conversation is much less embarrassing than not meeting the deadlines that would force partners to have to apologize to clients.

12. Engagements with clients in new industries are great opportunities and you should seek these out. On new clients, you should read the previous years' financial statements, research the industry on the Internet, obtain industry profile reports from or run some numbers on www. profitcents. com.

13. If you need to do some type of work you've never done before, look it up to obtain a familiarity and then ask for some assistance in **understanding your initial approach.**

14. Plan the work before you start. Write out a brief work plan for that day for yourself and your staff. Go to the client organized, prepared and ready to work. Also, showing your staff that you are prepared creates confidence in you.

15. For your own starting point on something new – start with cash. Check out the bank reconciliation. It always worked for me. You see the cash that comes in and cash that goes out. What else do you really need to understand about the client? Let your charge do the other testing. They will love you for not making them do cash and you'll have the handle on the client.

——— ——— ———

I received many calls about this question. I find it important that there is concern about a staff person's well being. The better the staff do, the better it will be for your firm.

In relooking at it, I think it is important for partners to consider the careers of their staff and be part of those careers' successful management.

I suggest that anyone having staff read this question and the response carefully and consider how their staff are progressing, developing and adapting to changing roles and responsibilities. Each staff person is an investment and that investment shouldn't be looked at as a passive investment on automatic pilot – rather it should be managed actively.

The dividends come with the growth of the staff and hopefully with their becoming partners or successors some day. Your concern should be transferred into positive action.

18. Three and a Half Ways to Get into Your Own CPA Practice

Q:

I am working for a CPA firm, but would like to get into my own practice. Can you give me some suggestions?

A:

Essentially, you have three options (four if you count my pet project, but I won't belabor it).

1. Buy a practice

> Any practice you buy should provide about half of your necessary current income.
>
> The remainder of your needed income should be financed by your savings or loans.
>
> You need to set up a plan to meet with people who can either become clients, or refer clients to you. From what I've seen, most

people will build their practice to a point where they are making a living no later than the end of the second year of being in business.

An alternative to personal door knocking is to advertise. However, that needs a skill few have. I have not seen too many CPA ads that have generated revenue, but I've seen enough to know that the right advertising program works and produces new clients. Most of the CPA firm ads are announcements of their being there, goodwill ads, yellow page or Internet site ads, or branding ads. Advertisements should be designed to get business leads. My experiences in advertising have included complete failures with some methods, and tremendous successes with others. Some of my ads have not produced immediate success, but have yielded profits because of the longevity of the clients obtained through the advertising. Also, be aware that advertising is not marketing – it is one part of an overall marketing program.

To support yourself, you can try to get some per diem work; however, this will take you away from the marketing that I feel is necessary to get your practice up to your break-even living level. The per diem will add time to any growth target.

Consider the shortfall in your "salary" your investment in the practice. And keep my two-year target in sight, and work at it.

There is a difficulty in buying a practice if you have no experience running a business that buying the franchise (see next item) eliminates. A sizable side practice will provide the confidence the seller will need to trust you for the balance of the purchase price.

2. Buy a tax preparation franchise

There are many available and these can provide reasonable income and entree into business. This method is a single path to a segment of the CPA business, but it is a start and will allow plenty of time after tax season to market your other areas of expertise. Many people think that having a "storefront" for a business location eliminates other methods of soliciting business such as knocking on doors or asking for referrals. It doesn't, it just is another and easier way to get tax return clients.

3. Start from scratch with clients you moonlighted with

And if you have no clients, then what makes you think you can get clients to develop your practice? Work per diem a maximum three days a week – you'll need the other days to do work, network and get business.

Use your moonlighted clients as a base to merge into an established practice.

3 ½. Buy a CPA practice franchise

I think this can be very effective, if they exist.

My idea of a retail location that will perform full service accounting work is the "Accounting Store. "

This idea is to start a storefront full service CPA practice. I've had the idea for many years and have suggested it to quite a few young accountants, but no one ever tried it. If you think you would like to try it – contact me and I'll share what I've put together.

14 Techniques To Get Your First Clients In A New Practice

1. Call or speak to everyone you know to let them know you just started your practice and would appreciate any referrals.

2. And give them either two or three business cards,

3. or a simple flyer with your contact information and qualifications and/or services performed.

4. If some of the people you know are in business, instead of calling, stop in at their office; tell them you were passing by or saw someone in the area; and tell them the "good news" about your practice, and would appreciate any referrals or business opportunities. Don't spend more than 10 minutes with them – you dropped in unexpectedly and shouldn't take them away from what they were doing for more than 10 minutes.

5. For attorneys, call and tell them you would like to stop by for 10

minutes, ask when and then tell them the "good news. "

6. Also, contact everyone you've ever met.

7. Don't overlook bankers. Contact every one you ever met. Mostly they won't be able to help you, but out of 25 bankers you should get at least one referral for something.

8. Other types of people that can refer business are insurance agents, financial planners, business brokers, other accountants particularly from larger firms and from firms you worked for, owners of restaurants you are known at (yes, I've gotten clients this way), and copier and scanner salespeople. Do you get the idea…? Everybody you have ever had contact with.

9. Join Chambers of Commerce and networking groups and attend every meeting. Your frequent attendance will make people depend on seeing you. This is when someone knows he or she will see you and he or she could casually bring up a matter without incurring an obligation. When people call with a question, they could feel there is some sort of "obligation" even if it is to explain why they need the answer or why they are not going forward with you; but at a networking meeting it is a no-obligation exploratory conversation.

10. Use your contacts as currency. When you make referrals of your clients to someone, make sure they appreciate why you selected them and ask them to keep you in mind if they can refer something to you.

11. I don't think it is necessary to see people for breakfast or lunch, unless you know them well and they've already referred business to you.

12. Set up an email message to send to your referrers. You can establish a blog (with WordPress such as I have) but to reach your list directly, you should email them the posting. Make your blogs short – not longer than the Gettysburg Address, and send them as BCC (blind copies). This way you know they get it – for blogs they need to sign up for and many won't do that. I've had people contacting me with referrals who I believe only thought of me at that moment because of the email from me.

13. Find something to postal-mail your contacts and always write a

personal note. You can send reprints of articles you wrote, articles you wrote that were not published but can be presented in a similar format, newspaper and magazine articles, books, a newsletter, or something related to their hobby or individual interests. Try to do this at least once every six weeks. FYI, many times I buy multiple copies of a magazine or newspaper and rip out the article I want to send. Doing this makes it look like I personally sent them my copy from my newspaper or magazine and that it is not a "mass-produced" mailing.

14. I try to call people or send an email on their birthday. This has lost some effect since Facebook now reminds people of their friends' birthdays. However, I still like to do this and in some cases, it gives me an opportunity to speak with someone I've been out of touch with.

19. Improving Quality Control

Q:

I want to improve my firm's review and quality control. Do you have any suggestions?

A:

This is a recurring issue for most firms. Every CPA practice needs quality control. The issue is whether a dedicated quality control ("QC") person is needed, and if not, how the QC can be done without one.

A practice is a business and every business must be run efficiently and profitably. QC is an area that I have found many firms getting tied up in and spending either nothing or much more than they should.

A firm needs a dedicated QC person when the workload volume warrants it, especially where there are bottlenecks and backlogs because the supervisor or partner who would review the work is not readily or easily available; the scheduling becomes exceedingly difficult; and the expertise and training becomes more specialized and wider in scope.

Almost every larger size firm has dedicated audit, attestation and financial statement report QC people; some even maintain firewalls between the QC and the audit staff. Virtually every tax return, no matter how small, is reviewed by someone – whether it is a reviewer, another preparer, their supervisor or a partner.

This question is not whether it is being done, but whom and should it be a separate QC person.

There are different ways of establishing QC methods and procedures. Depending on the underlying quality of the original work, measures have to be established to assure the best quality at the least cost. The lowest cost always comes where the person first performing the service does it correctly. The QC person, who is usually at a higher level and billing rate, would spend a minimal amount of time and the product gets delivered quickly and profitably. If the first-level work is done carelessly and without interest, then the reviewer will practically have to redo the work – either through extensive notes, comments and discussion, or simply making the corrections to get the work done.

QC starts with the processes and determination of the firm to assure the best job possible gets done at the lower levels. Part of this is the right procedures and checklists and a resolve that they are adhered to. Another part is the ego and pride of the staff to do the best job possible, complete as much of their work as they can, and not leave open items for their boss or the QC people to clean up. A "doing it right the first time" culture has to permeate the firm. With that, the QC person can spot check the work and focus in on the major issues, using the saved time to add value to the assignment and train and further develop the staff. Otherwise, the QC time is spent redoing and correcting errors, carelessness and just plain apathetic work, which wears out the reviewer and forecloses any meaningful training and development.

The person performing the QC needs to have the authority to enforce fully the processes and procedures, and should not be expected to correct the work. Having the person making the errors correct them establishes a pattern of quality always, training and continuous learning, and of not settling.

In most businesses, error rates of more than 8% to 10% are totally unacceptable, while in an accounting firm, error rates of as "low" as those percentages are unheard of and considered great. A QC person is necessary, but not as an added person on the project.

QC starts with the first person touching a file. They need to be taught to follow the procedures without shortcuts, and to self-check their work before it is handed in for review. There is very little that a person does in audit and attestation and financial statement work, or tax compliance that cannot be self-checked and proved. Another self-checking mechanism is to have them learn (your job is not to teach, but for them to learn!) to apply a reasonableness test. The completed work should be looked at to see if the purposes requiring the work and procedures were met; if the results make sense; what the client would look at; and whether the user would spot anything out of order. A mindset is needed to apply a critical analysis of the completed product.

Finding a QC person is not that easy. Besides technical expertise, the reviewer needs the ability to focus in on major issues; recognition they shouldn't get bogged down with details; value of their time; and training skills, patience and the ability to communicate the errors they find in a way that trains and elicits buy-in, growth and the elimination of future errors of the same type.

20. Talking Too Much Trying to Get a Client

Q:

I usually give away too much info at a meeting to get a new client. We simply answer too many of their questions during the initial meeting.

We don't know how much info to give away so the possible new client will get hooked and not take the information and run to somebody else. Usually the somebody else is cheaper. How do I find the right balance?

A:

Frank always complained to me that I did the same thing. I don't think I gave away too much info as I presented the impression that I was an "expert" in everything, which no one can be. That lessened my importance as someone who could handle his or her issues, reducing my own and my firm's value. After time, I held back by saying that their question was something that Peter or Frank, or someone else from my firm was expert in and would handle for them, when (never say "if") we are engaged.

21. Hiring an Experienced Person

Q:

We were looking for an additional experienced person and hired someone with five years experience.

But she said she couldn't start until January 3rd. She said she had work she had to finish up. Two days before Christmas she called to tell me her firm made her a "better" offer and she decided to stay there.

It now appears that we will be entering our busy season short a person. This seems to happen a lot. What do you suggest?

A:

You have a common problem. You also "invest" too much in looking for an experienced person where your chance of getting someone suitable is not good.

First of all, you are hiring someone of questionable ability. You will only know what they can do after they are working for you a while.

Second, you are hiring someone who was not happy where they were. What makes you think they will be happy with you?

Maybe they were unhappy because:

1. They felt they were not progressing as well as they should or weren't given opportunities to grow and develop further.

If that is the case, why are you hiring them at either the level they were at or a higher level ? Chances are they didn't learn everything they should have for that level – that's what they told you. Aren't you listening?

2. They weren't permitted to specialize or become an expert and take the CPE they needed to. See previous bullet point.

3. They weren't adequately compensated. That is possible, but how long did it take them to realize that and leave? And if they waited a while, how much enthusiasm did they bring to their job? And if they started looking to leave right away, what makes you think their boss did not anticipate this and decide they did not want that person?

4. You might be hiring an unhappy person.

Danger signals:

> • They have not passed the CPA exam;
> • They have an unexplained time gap in their resume;
> • They got stuck in a place and remained there too long (you define "too long");
> • They did not supervise staff – maybe not able to, or not given opportunity – and if you will provide that opportunity, how much will they pay you for that?

Don't give a raise from their present pay level, but promise to re-evaluate it in six months, and make sure you keep your promise.

If they are returning to public accounting perhaps they left because they didn't like it. If they realized they made a mistake after a short period they might work out. If they want to return after nine years, then give me a break.

5. It was their first job, and realized it wasn't for them, but stayed a year or two to learn as much as they could so they would be prepared for the next level. This could be a good person and they could be right on the mark because this frequently occurs in smaller firms. However, you will be hiring someone with two years of bad experience or training. Why?

6. There is an exception, and that is that the firm they were working for had to lay off some staff. If that is the case, then you might be getting a real star, so pursue it. One way to "test" that is to see their work history. Did they have five jobs in 10 years, or one or two jobs? I would stay away from the person with five jobs.

The solution:

My solution is simple, but not so simple: Hire people out of school and train them properly in your systems, procedures, techniques, style and methods.

This way you won't have to settle on what's available. If you don't do this, think about your reality. On some basis, what you have been doing isn't working, so consider trying something new – something that the largest and most successful CPA firms have always done – hire people out of school! It is not so simple because most small firms don't want to hire people just out of school because they don't want to train them or spend the time training and in many cases, they may not know how to train. This puts you in a bind – between a rock and a hard place. Well, that's the problem, isn't it? And you decide to "solve" your problem the same way all the time – hiring "experienced" people. Why not try the other way – the way that works for all the successful firms in our profession?

Oh, back to the specifics of the question. If you hired out of school and trained them your way, you wouldn't have to put up with hiring people who "can't start" yet.

I have a training method that has worked for me for 50 years. I call my training method, the Ed Mendlowitz Training Method or the 30:30 Training Method. I had lunch recently with Christine Booth, a CPA who, after listening to my method, said she knows what I mean and calls it her "Learning to Cook with My Grandmother" method.

The 30:30 Training Method is available as a downloadable PDF ebook at cpaclick.com/30-30-book. Use the page number at the bottom of this page as a discount code to buy it for half price.

Footnote: The expression "between a rock and a hard place" originated in the late 15th century by John Morton, Archbishop of Canterbury, who was also the tax collector. He reasoned that anyone living modestly must be saving money, so they could afford to pay taxes; and someone living extravagantly was obviously rich so they could afford taxes. This expression is also called "Morton's Fork."

22. Adding Family Office Services

Q:

Some of my clients are getting older and are becoming unable to handle their own financial affairs and I have been asked if I could assist them. What is involved and how do I charge for it?

A:

Many large firms provide "family office" services. This is a complete one-stop financial service that helps clients manage their money, pay their bills, collect their dividends and interest, and make sure insurance isn't cancelled, mortgage, car lease or condo fee payments aren't skipped, and tax payments paid on time.

Following is a sample engagement letter that I use with clients needing such services that provides a detailed description of what the service involves. Depending upon the client I call it family office services or bookkeeping services, or both, but the work is basically the same with family office a higher level service involving review of investments and similar activities.

Sample Engagement Letter for Family Office Services

Date

Client's name and address

RE: Outsourced bookkeeping services

Dear _____ ,

We are pleased to provide you with this proposal of family office outsourced bookkeeping services that we will perform for you.

Outsourced Bookkeeping Services

We will serve as your internal family office/outsourced bookkeeping office to include the following services:

These services will include you individually, the trusts you established where you are trustee, and your _____.

We will establish a computerized secure cloud based accounting and bookkeeping system suitable for you. This will include a review of your accounting and bookkeeping needs and configuration of an accounting system for you using appropriate software.

We will set up the chart of accounts, prepare recurring entries and memorized transactions, and configure the program to provide the reports and information that would best serve your needs.

Periodically, you will send us your bills for checks to be prepared and sent out. Ideally, we will directly receive all your bills and ascertain their validity and accuracy. Note that we will pay your bills without prior approval from you unless we think it is necessary. You will have an opportunity to review everything we paid once a month. At that time, we could make adjustments or request adjustments from your vendors.

We will write and mail checks for payments due by you in a timely manner. Generally, we will review all items on a weekly basis and perform whatever is necessary. Checks for amounts in excess of a minimum amount, e. g. $5,000, with the exception of the monthly recurring expenses, real estate taxes, income taxes and estimated tax payments will not be paid by us without your advance approval.

We will download all credit card transactions into the accounting system.

We will enter the payroll information for household or other employees employed by you from the payroll prepared by the payroll service including recording the tax payments. We will also review the quarterly and annual payroll tax returns that will be prepared by the payroll service.

We will review income you are supposed to receive and ascertain that it is received or deposited timely. This will include all amounts you usually receive or should receive. Note: Most of the collection and depositing of income receipts will be done by you with the information sent to us to record and track.

We will record receipt of income and deposits, and track amounts that are expected to be received.

We will review receipts for medical expenses and prepare the necessary forms for reimbursements, and follow up on their payment.

We will maintain electronic files of the original invoices and receipts in our office.

We will prepare sales and use tax returns (if applicable).

We will prepare annual Forms 1096 and 1099 information returns for submission to the taxing authorities and distribute them to independent contractors, if any, and if necessary.

We will maintain insurance, financial and tax calendars to make sure critical items are timely paid.

We will work with your insurance agents to make sure you have current policies.

Reports provided

We will send you by email monthly a listing of all disbursements and receipts along with copies of all invoices and bills. This will generally be sent by the end of the first week of each month.

We will send you by email copies of all bank reconciliations monthly, usually within one week of receiving the bank statements, along with a copy of the bank statements.

We will reconcile all brokerage and fund accounts and send copies to you. We will arrange to receive copies directly from the brokerage firms and banks as applicable, or be granted online access

Monthly balance sheets and income statements in the form of a trend analysis to be discussed with you via telephone every month.

We will always have available for your review a year-to-date general ledger. We will provide it as you request. Generally, we will send these to you at six-month intervals.

You will have 24/7 access via the cloud to review everything done on your behalf.

Other services

Provide secretarial services as needed.

Arrange for temporarily investing excess cash.

Telephone calls and email messages or updates to you as necessary.

All other bookkeeping services as the needs arise.

Bank account information

We will not use a bank account in your name. We will open a separate checking account in our name for your funds and transactions. You would send us a check for an estimated two months expenses made out to us, as trustees for you. This amount would be replenished bimonthly after the first check.

We will not deposit any of your income into our account. Rather, all income will be deposited into accounts that you control and where we are not signatories. The only exception might be the automatic deposit of monthly recurring items that are transmitted to your accounts.

Software system

We will use QuickBooks, Quicken and other appropriate software for these services. The versions we will use will be licensed to us and will not be billed to you, unless the software providers change their policy and require us to purchase separate software packages for use in our servicing your work (which appears unlikely). We intend to order preprinted checks and these will be billed to you. Initially, we will print a limited number of checks in our office for you so that there would be no delay in getting started.

Control and oversight

All disbursements we make will be subject to the approval and other controls we have established. However, in making those disbursements, we will be relying on the accuracy and reliability of information provided. We will not audit, examine or review the information, other than to review them for reasonableness and compare them to previous transactions or such other documentation we have been provided with.

We will electronically scan and properly store in a paperless environment all correspondence, invoices, bills and worksheets in files to be maintained in our system with the same controls, safeguards and security. These records will always be available to you immediately upon your request. If you desire, we can grant you a password to access these files from your computer at your convenience.

We will be fully responsible for our personnel training and the timely performance of their work. We anticipate using the same people; however, on occasion we will vary the personnel so we could be assured of sufficiently trained backup personnel should it be necessary to use someone not regularly working on your records. There will be at least two additional people in our firm familiar with your system, needs and requirements.

We anticipate that someone from our firm will be working on your bookkeeping at least once a week. The number of hours will vary based upon the services required.

You are not hiring a person; you are engaging a firm with the levels of the expertise you will need. You will have *full-time availability at part-time prices*.

Avoidance of duplication of efforts

In order to avoid duplication of efforts, unnecessary costs and multiple payments for the same items we suggest that a hold be put on disbursements, checks, wire transfers and stock and security transaction orders from all your bank and brokerage accounts unless there are letters signed by you and a second person designated by you. You will no longer be writing checks and making disbursements, except to us in accordance with our agreement.

The transfers to us would be done by wire transfers directed by a letter signed by you.

Additionally, two signatures would be required to execute security and banking transactions including purchases and sales of securities.

Your present method of making charges to your credit cards will not be affected by our arrangement.

Benefits to you

We run the traditional side of your bookkeeping and finances so you can work on the unique things you do, or to lessen the pressure of your handling what seems to be a steadily increasing flow of paperwork.

We not only take a burden from you, we give you time – time to do what you do best and want to do and time that frees your mind from routine repetitive functions.

We give you an immediate turnkey operation with no waiting to get started.

Services not covered

Please note that outsourced bookkeeping services specified in this letter will not include the audit or review of any financial statements.

Please also note that our outsourced bookkeeping engagement cannot be relied upon to disclose errors, irregularities or illegal acts, including fraud or defalcations that may exist. However, we will inform you of any material errors that come to our attention and any irregularities or illegal acts that come to our attention.

Fees

There is a one-time set-up fee of $_____.

Our fee will be $_____ per hour for outsourced bookkeeping services, $_____ per hour for partner review and oversight, plus a $_____ per month supervisory/administrative/facility fee. After the first year, when we have a better idea of the scope of the work, we will quote a fixed fee if you so desire. Additionally, we will bill you for out-of-pocket disbursements including postage and delivery services.

Fees are payable as billed. We will write our check on or near the 10th of each month for the previous month's charges. There will be an additional charge of 1. 5% per month for past due amounts. Also, should you hire any of our personnel it is acknowledged that we would be entitled to a $25,000 "search" fee.

You may discontinue the services from us at any time. In that event, our services to you would cease immediately, or continue until such time as mutually agreed upon including the appropriate fee. We will also issue a final invoice for unbilled work within a reasonable time, thereafter.

Confidentiality

Professional standards preclude us from disclosing client information without your specific consent.

Conclusion

We are most pleased that you are considering us for these services. Please call me to discuss this proposal and any additional questions you may have. If the above meets with your approval, please sign a copy and return it to us.

Cordially,

_____, CPA

This letter correctly sets forth my understanding of your engagement:

_____

23. Terrible Service and Failure of Management

This is not a question, but a story and comment.

One Sunday evening my wife and I went into a reasonably upscale restaurant and we had terrible service from everyone we interacted with.

When we were seated, the table wobbled and we asked if they could do something or move us to another table. Ten minutes later, someone showed up with a wad of napkins that made it worse. Five minutes later, they asked if we were OK, and put us at another table. Ten minutes after that they took our order, but we asked for some drinks right away, which we only got after we complained to the manager.

We were given some rolls, but no butter or oil, which came with the salads about 10 minutes after we got our drinks. We then asked for some water, which came when the main course was served 20 minutes after we finished our salads. We used up the oil and asked for some more, which never came.

We ran out of time and could not order coffee or dessert, and asked for the check, which came fairly quick but after sitting there with my credit card sticking out of the folder for 10 minutes we asked the manager to ring it up so we could get out of there and get on with our lives, which certainly were not enhanced by the lousy dining experience.

One consolation: the manager treated us to the drinks. Also, the food was very good, except my wife asked for one change in the order and it wasn't done. The way I see it, they lost a customer, lost the payment for the drinks, lost the sale for coffee and dessert.

And it wasn't just one server who stunk – it was five different people, including the manager.

As a business consultant and observer, I place the blame on management, which started with their hiring unmotivated people. The entire culture was inattention to the needs of the customer or a lack of recognition of what the restaurant's role was and why people went there. I seriously doubt that restaurant will remain open, but I don't care because I will never go back there again.

Now, my question to you:

Do you treat your clients, i. e. customers the way that restaurant treated my wife and me, or is everyone in your firm committed to providing exceptional service and an extremely pleasant experience?

You can personally be committed to this, but if it isn't transmitted to your staff with that same attitude adopted by all of them, you will not retain your clients or generate the maximum revenues possible from them.

This attitude is called culture, and it applies to everyone. The person answering the phone after four or five rings, or sounding short-tempered, or an admin person inadvertently folding over the edge of the back cover of the report or tax return, or the postage meter indicia or address label placed crookedly on the envelope all create bad impressions.

Now, really bad impressions are created when you miss a deadline, spell the client's name wrong, send the report to a previous address, fail to return the clients' original data or provide journal entries before you are asked for them. All of these actions ensure you will not maximize your revenues.

Now ask yourself how you handle your clients. Do you copy that lousy restaurant or respond the way clients expect to be treated?

A deadline is a promise and a missed deadline means you lied. Keep your promises and get your work done on time.

You need a team behind you to expand your practice.

You could be the best there is as far as the client is concerned, but if a partner or manager neglects to respond to that client that way the client expects, your image will be tarnished. What I have found is that clients won't necessarily drop you because of inattentive staff or team members since they like you so much or they remember the great thing you did for them 17 years ago, but they won't recommend you.

So your great work and personal relationship keeps the client, but your inattentive staff loses the additional services your firm could have done for that client, the delegation you need so you could grow, and that client as a referral source for you.

24. Fee Increases

Q:

I haven't raised my fees in three years. How do I suddenly go about it now and how much should I raise them?

Also, I have many business clients where the individual returns are done as part of the yearly service without extra billing. How can I start charging for this?

A:

Since you haven't increased your fees in three years, you have to be losing ground financially.

I suggest you increase every fee, effective January 1, by 5% (or any percentage of your choosing). The only exceptions I would make would be for clients barely hanging on. When you increase the fee, do it for the exact amount, not rounded.

For example, if a client is paying $425.00 per month, the increase should be $21.25 making the new fee $446.25. Bringing it up to a round number will make the increase greater than 5%.

Rounding it down will cost you current revenue and will reduce the future base that increases will work off of.

If clients complain, they really won't be seriously considering dropping you, but will want to try to get the increase waived.

A simple understandable response is that you were falling behind and needed to raise everyone 5%, and could not have any exceptions. This works, and the reality is that you are falling behind and this small increase per client will help you balance out this year's increased costs.

You lost out on recouping your previous years' increased costs, but you shouldn't forgo this anymore. You can print the following notation on the bottom of each bill sent out for the first time with the increase. "Due to increased costs, your monthly (or quarterly or annual) fee has been increased 5% effective with this bill. " Alternatively, send a form letter indicating that your fees will be increased 5% with the New Year (or effective July 1, or any other date based on when you start).

As to the 1040s you don't charge for, a suggestion is to tell clients that it is becoming increasingly difficult to justify to the IRS when there is an audit, not charging separately for the owner's individual tax returns.

The IRS will impute part of the fee to the owner's tax return and it will end up costing them additional tax since the tax preparation fee would fall into the "non-deductible" 2% threshold on their personal tax returns.

Accordingly, you will start charging for this tax season a nominal fee of $150 or $200, or whatever you think is appropriate for the individual returns you do.

Keep in mind that if a client has three children living at home and they all get returns, and two of them have income from three different states, your costs are substantial for that client. This fee arrangement will reduce your "losses" on this.

25. Merging Your Practice

Q:

I asked you what I should do about merging and I haven't gotten a specific answer from you. Please, Ed, what should I do?

A:

I can't give you an answer. I can give you a process to follow that should provide your answer.

Actually, this works and I've gotten good feedback from many colleagues. I've also rethought it many times, and still think this is the way to go about it.

Write out what you really want for yourself and your practice. Jot down your "ideal" situation – it is your piece of paper – fantasize and put down your wildest dreams, professionally that is.

Look at what you wrote and convert it to a plan for the next few to five years.

Think about starting to implement the plan. Take the first step.

If merger is part of your plan, then start figuring the type of person you would like to "get in bed with" and then work toward that.

If a merger is not part of your plan, or not something you really want to do, then drop the idea and work out your practice's plan that will now have to include moving, expanding, contracting or doing whatever needs to be done. This will probably mean doing some things you will find unpleasant, but most likely you will have no choice in the matter, and you might as well get to it. Your choice could end up being to pick the least offensive. Keep in mind that these are business decisions and try to think impassively even though you might be setting your course for the next few years.

Actually, your future can be a somewhat exciting blank slate with the starting point where you sit right now. Alternatively, it could be an albatross around your neck and drag you down. It's your choice. Excitement and growth, or settlement with discontent. I hate to use a cliché, but when you stop growing, you die!

If there is a concern about what would happen to your practice if there were a premature death, then you should enter into a practice continuation agreement. If you still haven't done anything, do it. If you want a sample agreement, see my "drop dead" info at the appendix at the end of this book. .

One way to get going is to make a large T on a page and list the goods on one side and bads on the other.

You need to be clear on what you want and what is good for you. If you are not clear, then you will flounder.

26. Selling Practice to Staff

Q:

I am nearing retirement and want to sell my practice to two longtime staff people, but they don't get along, and I am afraid to sell to them. What should I do?

Second Question: I have a large individual tax practice, but also have an audit practice that is handled by different staff in my firm. How do I sell this practice? None of the larger buyers wants the tax clients and none of the smaller buyers wants the audit clients.

A:

Both questions raise the same issue: The practice is not generally salable to one person. However, they get different responses from me.

First question response: In the first instance with two employees, divide the clients into two groups and offer it to them in that way. Let them decide if they want to be partners, or whether each will want to buy half (or however you divvy it up). Tell them you will want a down payment with a payout for the balance. There are some dangers here. One is that one, or both, can decide to "steal" your clients and go into business for themselves. Another danger is that only one will want to buy and they couldn't handle the entire practice alone. Another danger is that your division might not be completely acceptable with one or more clients "belonging" to the other group. Also, if there are staff it will be harder to divide up the staff, especially if they work on both groups of clients.

Some have suggested an employment agreement prohibiting "stealing" clients or setting a purchase price for stolen clients that will protect you. It will protect you much better than if there weren't an agreement, but it will only be as good as your willingness to enforce breaches by suing. Also, getting an agreement signed now is a little like fixing the gate after the horses ran away. These agreements should be part of your hiring procedures.

Second question response: Split up the clients and staff and sell it to two separate people. This should be easier to bundle than the above practice since there would be no tip-off to the staff and a much lower risk of loss. Presenting it to the clients would be more difficult than if one person acquired the entire practice, but should be managed satisfactorily if the buyers are experienced in taking over practices.

27. ■ Staff Who Do Not Listen

Q:

My staff doesn't listen to me.

To be able to manage and control my business I need them to prepare a monthly schedule of what they plan to do that month. I further need to know each morning if they did what they were supposed to do the previous day, and whether there was anything not done, or anything extra that wasn't planned on. My problem is that they don't give me the schedule and then don't call or email me to tell me what they did. I really need to know this stuff and can't figure out how to get them to do it.

What can you suggest?

A:

I can spend a couple days on this, and I did have two phone calls, each lasting almost an hour with the practitioner who called me.

What To Do

1. "My staff doesn't listen to me. " This is the starting point. You need to recognize who's the boss. Ask yourself: "Who's the boss?" And see how you feel about the reality of it.

2. In general, the staff people are the "bosses. " This is true in the sense that they do what they want, and not what they ought. In some cases, it is amazing that much gets done in these firms. Unchecked staff left to their own decisions, will do what is easiest, less complicated, most comfortable or least confrontational. On the other hand, the boss needs the most important project done first, followed by the second, and then third and so forth.

3. In professional practices, staff need to be managed. Not micromanaged in the areas of their professional expertise and ability, but in many cases, micromanaged in how they choose to spend their time. Their professionalism will dictate how they will handle a situation, how much time to commit to it, when to seek assistance, when to call it quits on a project, and when to decide if enough has been done or if they've reached the point of rapidly diminishing returns. It is professional judgment, creativity and expertise that need freedom. However, what clients are worked on and when and for how long needs strong control. That is the firm's inventory and needs careful management. In most cases what is to be done should be predetermined, planned and should work off a budget determined by the client and partner. Because of the high level of certain staff, much freedom is extended for self-management or direction, but it still needs accountability. Thus, the monthly schedules and daily status updates.

4. It is not usually an isolated instance when staff doesn't respond and comply with the scheduling and accountability procedures. There are most likely other things they won't be doing, such as the proper completion of audit and other work process checklists, circumventing supervision procedures, not keeping up to date such as the timely review of journals they subscribe to, short-cutting work that needs to be done for clients and inattention to CPE programs.

5. Non-complying staff is either the fault of their managers or a lack of something in themselves, or both. If there were isolated instances within a firm, then I would blame the staff people. However, if it were widespread, then I would have to blame the managers or partners.

6. I recommend getting rid of staff who thwart the management controls the firm needs. No control means no growth, lower profits and the inevitable leaving of those people at some point and usually at a time of their choosing, which can be at a bad time for you. This is hard, but your focus needs to be what is best for the business in the long range. Retaining such people is a bad decision.

7. I suggest that one reason staff don't follow through on administrative things they need to do is their awareness that the partner does not look at it, or question anything or follow through on what they need to do with the information provided. Repeatedly ignoring the submissions results in noncompliance. Think about your role, or lack of role, in this process. If it is important, then you should be on top of it regularly, if not daily.

8. I know, you say you are too busy to look at it daily. What about weekly? Or do you give it a cursory glance monthly or when a problem arises? If it is important, then make it important! Make it your job to control your "inventory. "

9. Oh, you don't want to spend the hour or so a day? Then hire someone to do it. Maybe add it to the duties of your secretary or an administrative person. Work out what needs to be done.

What Needs To Get Done

1. Each staff person prepares a suggested monthly schedule three days before the beginning of the month.

2. A partner or senior manager reviews the entire schedule with each staff person discussing what will be done, why, budget requirements, deadlines, carryovers of work not done, and what wasn't scheduled, and why.

3. At the end of each day the staff person will send a brief email or fax affirming scheduled work that was done, listing anything that wasn't done, anything extra they did, any carryover work and when it will be done, impending deadlines, and anything they want to call to their supervisor's or partner's attention.

4. Each morning by 10 a. m. , the admin person will review the daily reports and compare it against the work that was scheduled, will make sure unperformed services are scheduled, and find out why additional work was done and whether it should be billed. A brief summary should be prepared and discussed with a partner – that morning.

5. The partner should review the results with the admin person each morning, either in person or by phone, to determine the adherence to the schedules and to make necessary decisions. If a staff person needs to be spoken with, they should be contacted at that time. It is important and necessary for the staff to see the follow-through and resolve of the partners.

6. People who don't comply need to be spoken to, and continued noncompliance should lead to dismissal.

28. ◼ Client Survey

Q:

Is there any value to sending clients a survey?

A:

Yes. Our firm sends a survey with every deliverable to a client. We want to know what they think and how they feel about our service. I think your best friends are the clients who complain. This gives you an opportunity to correct any deficiencies, misperceptions or insufficiencies.

Once a longtime very good client put on the survey that we were great but our fees were high. I immediately met with him, reviewed our charges, had the time runs and details of everything extra we had been doing beyond the scope of our engagement, and the value to the client.

In the following year, he recommended two clients to us! I don't believe we would have gotten the referrals had he not complained.

You'll find a survey we use here: cpaclick. com/eds-client-survey.

29. Managing Client Meetings

Q:

I find I am spending more and more time at meetings with clients. Do you have any suggestions on how to limit the time?

A:

I used to have that problem. I solved it very simply.

I now prepare an agenda before I meet with the client. I list the new items we need to discuss, follow-up items from prior meetings, and a few blank lines to add new things the client may also want to discuss.

The items are listed in each area by most important first. I open the meeting by presenting the agenda to the client and asking him or her if there is anything to add. We then discuss briefly the order the client wants to discuss them in and just before we start, I tell the client that the meeting shouldn't take more than 45 or 50 minutes (or whatever time is necessary), setting a pace to the meeting. After I started this quite some time ago, my meetings became much more productive, efficient and enjoyable.

30. ■ Providing Work Papers to New Accountant

Q:

A longtime business client who owed me a large balance for unpaid fees sent a letter dropping me. He then wrote me a letter requesting me to send "his" papers to his new accountant.

Can I insist on being paid first or do I have to send the papers? I made some notes on a worksheet adjusting his numbers that went on the tax return. Do I have to send this also and if so, do I have to write these up in proper journal entry form?

A:

He has to send the papers that "belong" to the client, and cannot hold the papers hostage for payment. This includes all adjusting entries the CPA made when he prepared the business tax return.

Since he did not make actual journal entries, but did make notes that were used to adjust the numbers, those notes would be considered part of the client books that "belong" to the client and need to be sent to the client.

He does not need to do any additional work such as putting them in proper journal entry format as long as the notes could be followed by the new accountant. If there are other notations on the worksheets that do not affect the amounts on the return, he could cover those before he photocopies the worksheets.

This is tough stuff for the accountant. He needs to be more diligent collecting his money in the future. This is not an isolated instance. We all get stuck like this. It's a controversial and annoying issue and the CPA seems to lose no matter how you argue it, or what approach you want to take.

The general consensus I get is to give the papers and chalk it up to a bad experience, and try not to let it happen again.

31. ■ Consulting With a Client Who Is Also a Friend

Q:

I have a close friend who is also a client. He went through a rough time with his wife threatening a divorce and we spent a lot of time talking about it (out of office settings). I sent him a bill and he returned it with a notation that "we spoke as friends and not as a professional consultation, and the bill should be cancelled. " What should I do?

A:

Unless you want to lose the friend and client, forget about it.

The problem is that the conversations were during regular golf games, at lunches that are usual and various phone calls. If there were a professional service rendered or that should have been conducted, it should have been done in the office preceded with a comment that this would be billed extra. If the client did not want to pay or did not value or perceive a value from the service to be rendered, that is his prerogative, and the time then should not have been spent.

Once there is a clear understanding, you can then choose to bill it or not.

What I do after an initial meeting or two is tell the client that it seems like he will be needing ongoing consultations for advice, guidance or strategy, and I will bill him a minimum retainer and then will accumulate my time and will bill him additionally as things progress, with the hope that the retainer will be sufficient. I determine the retainer by assuming I will spend about 10 hours on the matter.

This happens a lot with the culprits being personal financial planning, retiring, paying for a child's college education, whether a client should buy a variable or immediate annuity, a potential bankruptcy, or short sale of a residence, or bringing in, or getting rid of a partner.

You have to draw the line between personal and professional activities. You also need to recognize that is how you make your living. You spend time and apply your knowledge and experience to individualized situations and need to be paid for it.

32. Serving on a Not-for-Profit Organization Board

Q:

I am on the board of directors and am treasurer of a not-for-profit organization. One of the board members is an officer of a commercial bank where we have our accounts. The organization wants to get a one-year CD with some excess funds they have. It turns out that the interest rate is less than half of what we could get from a local savings bank.

I suggested that we open the CD in the savings bank and the bank officer got very agitated and threatened to cut off the bank's support of the organization if we did not keep the funds in his bank. The bank is a substantial contributor to the organization, and I backed down.

Was I right?

A:

Yes. You need to look at the totality of the relationship. The amount contributed far offsets the lower interest you are earning. I would have a notation made in the minutes to this effect.

33. ■ Specialization

Q:

Can you recommend a specialty I can get involved in to generate more revenue for my practice?

Comment: My discussion with the CPA indicated that his practice consisted of a large individual tax return practice and many monthly business clients. He thought financial planning or business valuations would be a way to expand his services and make more money. It did not seem he had an intellectual interest in these areas.

A:

I told him to spend the time getting more business clients similar to what he had.

My reasons were:

> **1.** He wasn't interested in personal growth – just wanted to make more money.

> **2.** Both specialties he mentioned required obtaining designations that would require study and time – an investment he did not seem to want to make. I told him there was no pill he could take that would make him instantly adept in FP or BV, but if I heard of one, I would certainly let him know.

3. He did not seem to have an awareness of the scope of the specialties he mentioned. For instance, FP could include asset allocation assistance, budgeting consulting, retirement, education funding, estate or succession planning – all different specialties requiring different types of knowledge and training, and staffing. BV could include estate and gift valuations, buying a business analysis, due diligence, divorce valuations and forensic investigations.

4. He actually has a very good practice – whenever he got a new business client, his "annuity" income increased and went on and on and on. Getting a check every month is a pretty great business model.

5. FP or BV specialty work would require a large amount of his time. His present clients are primarily serviced by staff. He has about three or four meetings a year with each client. His time including client meetings and calls, supervision, training and review was about 25% of the total time servicing the client. He was using leverage and delegating work very effectively. If he went to the next level and invested in another staff person, he could probably reduce his time and possibly use the freed-up time to cross-sell clients some business advisory or consulting services (which is a specialty he should further inquire about). He could also examine his client base to see if he has a preponderance of clients in an industry, positioning himself as an "expert," and using that to perform additional services and in marketing for new clients.

6. FP and BV work are primarily one-shot assignments. Unless you sell product or manage money, the cost of getting new clients has to be covered by the work generated, which is very difficult without a critical mass of continual work being referred to him. With his present model, the acquisition cost is spread out over a period of time since the revenue stream from the client lasts for quite a while (many years based on his track record).
7. He did not have a critical mass of contacts to feed him FP or BV work and developing it would take "years" and substantial time and cost on his part.

8. In FP and BV niches, he would need to demonstrate an expertise such as writing articles or teaching CPE, which also would require large blocks of time.

9. His income was above average for the size practice he had. He also had quite a bit of time off in the summer and toward the end of the year. He indicated no interest in working harder – he said he wanted to work smarter on higher fee services. I told him that while he would receive higher hourly rates on the BV work, much of that work is time-sensitive, causing rushed conditions making it more difficult to schedule around his other commitments. If the BV expanded into forensic work, a lot of his time would be at the command of the attorneys he would be working with.

My conclusion was that he should spend more time trying to get additional business clients, and maybe try to upsell existing clients additional services.

34. Careless Staff

Q:

I have young staff preparing tax returns and there is a high degree of carelessness.

For example, one preparer entered the appraised value from the tax bill as the real estate taxes. Another filled out our tax payments worksheet but none of the numbers tied in to the amounts she put on the return. Yet another was missing information and did not indicate it when he handed in the return for review. None of these preparers looked at the output of the return they worked on.

Obviously, the reviewer caught these errors, but how can I stop them from occurring?

A:

This is a twofold problem for many firms.

> 1) The staff is not attentive to what they are doing. They do not consider the consequences of a lack of their care; and do not seem to have an internal pride that their work needs to be error-free. Some might even say they don't take "ownership" – meaning they think they are working on a piece of a project without any concept or responsibility of the whole or without a regard for what the client will get, see and be charged.

2) Your training is not transmitting what you expect. Many firms train on the technical matters without spending time to have staff understand the big picture.

Additionally, I find that staff members listen less than they should and managers talk more than they should. This fundamental issue is difficult to change with the great temptation of traditional methods thwarting alteration. My solution in dealing with this has been not to fight the inattention but to stop the excess instructions.

Another way to deal with the problem is to work on your overall processes and culture.

Regarding errors staff make and how the corrections should be dealt with, Joe Picone, a senior manager and the person in charge of staff development in my office sent me these comments:

"I know we have different opinions on whether the reviewer should make the changes or if you should make the preparer make the changes on a tax return…. and we can debate that some other time.

The biggest problem I have is when reviewers correct careless mistakes, but never show these careless mistakes or the consequences of these mistakes to the preparer. You need to call the staff out on it – you need them to feel bad about it and for them to see that it caused additional work for someone. I see this all the time in my position – a reviewer (sometimes even a partner) will show me something that a staff person did wrong. While I like to know these things and I feel it is important that I do know them, they still need to point them out to the staff. "

35. Marketing by New Staff

Q:

A young staff accountant wanted to know how he could bring in new business and clients.

A:

My answer was that he shouldn't be as concerned about bringing in business as he should be about planting seeds to be able to bring in business in the future.

Five Ways for a Young CPA to Network

1. By becoming active in one or two charitable or religious organizations working on specific projects and being an extra hand when needed. The object is to get involved and develop relationships

2. Developing and maintaining a list of everyone he knows and meets, and then finding ways to have at least a couple of contacts with them a year. I define a contact as any interaction – you can call them on their birthday, send them your firm's current newsletter issue with a personal note, mail them an article from a magazine or newspaper (I suggest postal mailing it, and not email), or send an

email to forward something about an activity of your firm.

3. Look for opportunities to mention your firm to clients and acquaintances.

4. Look for openings to bring additional service ideas to your supervisor's attention. People at clients' premises might mention things that they need or would like help with – this can present additional service opportunities for your firm.

5. Ask your supervisors, managers and partners questions on ways you can do things better when networking.

Networking is like growing a tree. It takes time to root, grow, develop and reach maturity. Allow at least five years for your contacts to take root. If you aren't getting any bites after five years with an organization or contact group you have been developing, examine what you are doing and seek assistance.

Be aware of the potential for business from the organizations you are considering becoming involved with. Consider the overall age of the people – you should seek out people who are your age or not more than five years older.

Consider if there are many other CPAs involved with that group and consider the general economic strata of the contacts – are they all blue-collar or entrepreneurs? Are they mid-level office staff or upper-level executives?

Assuming you have equal feelings toward two organizations, you should volunteer with the one that appears to have the greater potential.

36.

Recognizing a Value Pricing Opportunity

Q:

An accountant had a client who started a business eight years ago and used him for a couple of years until some big money was raised and they switched to a Big Four firm. He also stopped using the accountant for his personal return, switching to the Big Four firm.

He called the accountant last week to ask for assistance in evaluating a multimillion-dollar termination package. He needed to meet with the accountant right away since he did not want the offer to slip away. He then asked what the rates would be and could he have a discount since he was once a good client (he was – seven and eight years ago!).

Asking for a discount left a bad taste in the CPA's mouth and he called me. He wanted to know how to handle it. He felt he could bill $1500 to $2000 and wanted to do the work – it was interesting to him.

A:

After thinking about it an hour or so, I called him back and said he should ask for a $7,500 retainer upfront, and that he would present a bill when finished based on the value added to the transaction. I told him to explain that he was not charging for his time, but for the 30 years experience he had with many people in similar situations as well as also representing employers in these situations, and he fully understood the dynamics from both ends. He should say that if it were mishandled, it could cost him (client) hundreds of thousands of dollars between a lower payout, unfavorable and tenuous terms and timing and bad tax structuring. Further, the CPA should say that this work involved the highest skills he had; that it had to be handled on an "on demand" priority basis; the deal structuring wasn't work that could be delegated; and the tax structuring would be done by one of his partners who was a top tax expert in this field (or that he would run the tax plan by an outside employee compensation tax consultant to make sure nothing was missed). This was premium work and would be billed accordingly. Also, the client needed to understand that the fee was not relevant to the total transaction, he had only one shot at the best deal, and he shouldn't blow it by looking for a bargain basement accountant and fee.

I also told him not to chase this work if he couldn't get the retainer upfront. Note: Based on what he told me, I did not feel he would be able to get a larger retainer, so we settled on $7,500.

In the end, the accountant agreed with me and the client was told the above and also that a two- or three-hour meeting would not do justice to his situation and it needed a thorough analysis that could only be done based on the proposal just made to him. The CPA made a decision that a short meeting with many extra phone calls by the client would not be profitable and would be too disruptive to make it pay; and that he anticipated extra calls by the client trying to get the fee down. A follow-up call to me a week later told me he was very happy with the way he handled it, even though he didn't get the work. He also felt he was now better armed for future situations of a similar nature.

37.■Fire the Client

Q:

A client of 10 years was paying a fixed fee that is now a little less than half of our time charges.

Also, there had been a gradual scope creep with additional services being forced on us without any extra fees. The CPA had not received an increase in six years because of the client's constant complaining that the fee was too high. The client just told us they had a quote from another firm that was half of ours, and said if we didn't match it, they would leave us.

A:

I hate to advise accountants to drop clients, but in this case, there is no choice. There is no future with that client!

P. S. : When the CPA spoke with the new accountant it seems she was not told all the work that needed to be done – she will find out soon enough!

38. Collecting Past Due Fees

Q:

A client didn't pay his bills to me, doesn't return my phone calls and his secretary keeps sending me the tax notices he gets with notes of "when are you going to take care of them. "

I tell her that I need the client to call me before I can do any more work and she ignores this and keeps sending me the notices and other tax correspondence he gets. I don't want to tell him I am dropping him because then I don't think I'll ever be paid. Every year he goes on extension and he usually pays me half of what he owes when he sends me his tax info, but the past due amount has really accumulated to about three years of fees.

What should I do about getting paid?

A:

You have two choices:

> 1) I think you should send a certified letter informing him that you cannot do any more work until arrangements are made for him to pay his past due debt and the new work you will be doing.

2) Tell the client you need a check for the full current year's tax services before you can start working on his return, and need some payment on the back amounts.

Approach this as follows: Look at the past due amounts as dead, and just try to have the client not fall more behind, and if possible try to get something in any form toward the past due amount – for example charge $250, $500 or $1000 each month to his credit card toward the past due amounts.

With the past due amounts frozen, or on a small payment plan, getting paid in full for the current work should not be a burden to the client. You can also incentivize the on-account monthly payments by creating an understanding that when half or two-thirds of the past due balance is paid, you will cancel the remaining amount, or something similar to that.

Today the CPA is charging $600 a month to credit card and for the current year's fee, 50% when work comes in and 50% when return is completed.

39.■Value Pricing

Q:

I helped a client get a bank loan, negotiated the rate and fees with the bank and had a tight covenant loosened.

I prepared a personal financial statement, a compilation statement for the business, projected financial figures and accounts receivable projections and reviewed and discussed them with bank, and had numerous conversations with bank and client. Total time was six hours at $300 per hour.

It seems it was worth a lot more to the client than $1,800 — what should I bill?

A:

Prepare a detailed itemized bill for each service and charge what you think each separate item should be billed at.

Four items were separately listed on the bill totaling $7,000. Client thanked him for being so reasonable with the fees and wrote a check.

40.

Transforming From a Practice to a Business

Q:

A CPA sole practitioner with a few part-time staff told me that he has come to realize he no longer had a practice, but a business, and wanted to hire a person for "growth," not just someone to help him get through the day. He wanted some suggestions of what type of person he should hire.

A:

I suggested hiring someone just graduating and training him or her. He replied that he felt it would take too much time to train a newbie, and was leaning toward a more experienced person.

I pointed out that his big-picture view should be to become richer and work smarter, that he couldn't abdicate his management and review, and probably would need to provide at least the last 10% to 15% of a job to complete every job.

I seemed to convince him to try it my way. So he hired someone a little more mature, but who did not have CPA firm experience.

The results are not in yet, but I recommended a method that has worked for me, for my firm, for most larger practices, and all of the Big Four.

My training method is fully explained in a separate book. If you buy it, and read it, you can then call me to discuss any questions you have about the method.

41.■Past Due Fees

Q:

A client owes me a very large amount of money and seems to be giving me a runaround and I need to get the check quickly. The client has the cash, so that is not an issue.

Do you have any suggestions?

A:

Offer him a discount for immediate payment and tell him you will send a messenger to pick up the check, or he could deposit it in the firm's account.

When the accountant did as I suggested, the client paid the bill depositing it in the firm's account, and faxed the deposit slip to the accountant later that afternoon.

Another suggestion is to get the client's credit card info so they could get "points."

42. Below Normal Fee Assignments

Q:

We have a chance for a substantial special assignment, but at a very low rate – about 40% lower than our standard billing rates.

We need the revenue, want the client because there could be future work at better rates, there is good bragging rights and it looks good to the staff, but we don't want to lose money on it.

What do you suggest?

A:

Go for it!

The work is summer work when you are less busy, even with people on vacation, and you always have a summer intern eager to contribute. You will not need to hire anyone extra to work on the job, you will be busier and work harder than you normally would be, but you will be using resources that you are already paying for, with the exception of some overtime or bonuses. Basically, almost all of the entire fee will end up on your bottom line – you will have minimal cost, not your standard cost since you will be paying that anyway for seasonably reduced output.

43.Integrating an Acquired Practice

Q:

I bought a tax return practice in December from a person who was charging $180 per hour. My rate is $300 per hour so I did not make money and I would like to know what I could do to raise fees so I don't continue to lose on it.

A:

After a long discussion, it appears that he bought a good practice with good fees charged for the returns. His problem is that he has no employees and did all the work himself – about 750 tax returns – and was very overwhelmed with non-stop work.

Most of the level of work he did was for a person who typically would be billed at $120 per hour. So he was doing $120 hour level work, getting paid at $180 an hour and he is unhappy because he is not getting $300 an hour. His problem is that he has no leverage; has no one to pass most of the lower-level work on to; and had no fun working around the clock. However, he expects to retain about 80% of the clients because he met most of them and feels he established relationships with them.

So, I made a few suggestions…

Ten Tips to Managing
an Acquired Tax Practice

1. I told him that he is performing services beneath his level and should be thrilled he is realizing $180 per hour for the type of work he is doing. If he can't or doesn't want to hire someone at a lower level to do the work, then he should get past the thought that he is a $300-per-hour person and realize he is a $120-per-hour person getting paid $180.

2. I told him he should try to hire per diem people during tax season so he could have some relief.

3. He should spend a little less time with clients.

4. Try to do the return while they are sitting with him.

5. Next tax season he should keep this year's fee but tell the clients that he would increase fees 5% the following year (to cover increased costs, assuming it is the same type of return).

6. I also told him it seems that he purchased a winner and shouldn't do anything to screw it up.

7. He should call every client in the next month to touch base with them.

8. He should ask if there is any financial matter they need help with.

9. And he should point out that he has a CPA practice and does many other CPA type of services that they can consider him for or recommend him for.

10. He also told me he is studying to get his securities licenses and wants to offer financial products. I told him that the money spent to hire people to do the work is an investment that will enable him to spend the time doing what he thinks will be more lucrative work, and by having a staff person he will be elevated professionally in the eyes of his clients.

In the end, he sent me an email and said he already started making the phone calls and got some positive feedback.

44.

Timesheets or Not?

Q:

You seem to believe in value pricing, but still cling to the tradition of timesheets. Why?

A:

I believe timesheets are an essential part of any professional services organization. Some people contend that they should not be maintained since they should not be the basis of any pricing – that fees should be solely based on the value to the client. I disagree.

Even if we assume fees should be based solely on "value," time records provide an important role in information and control, and should be maintained.

One comment for firms that do not believe in time sheets is that you should do what you feel is the right thing for your practice and what works for you. In your case, this question is not for you.

13 Reasons to Get Better Value from Using Timesheets

1. Time records are a method of keeping track of costs. While information is entered at the billing rates, discounting it makes it into a cost system.

2. The information can be used for future scheduling; determining if work is done at the proper skill level; to identify who worked on the client and if someone not scheduled worked on the client it could lead to why they did; to determine if work was done that was not part of the prior agreed-upon engagement; or to just see how closely the actual work matched the budget.

3. Flex time and telecommuting have provided less visibility of staff, less hands-on review and discussions and fewer MBWA (Managing by Wandering Around) opportunities. Timesheets provide a means of tracking staff activities.

4. Time records provide a measurement of the type of work that is done in non-productive areas such as answering tax notices, preparing extensions or redoing work where the accountant didn't have all the information when she started.

5. Time records are a way to monitor client satisfaction by measuring work done correcting errors or on work that was redone.

6. An example of the benefit of keeping time records highlighted that a low-level tax department staff person worked on quite a few clients that she had no reason to work on. When we looked into it, we found that she was continually asked tax questions by mid-level audit staff because they got the answers they needed quickly, while the higher-level tax department people pushed these requests aside. This provided valuable information to evaluate the tax staff's interaction with the audit staff and enabled substantial changes that sped up the turnaround for those questions, and eliminated an oblique bottleneck.

7. Insightful information was found out when it was noticed that a high-level tax manager decided to lump all his tax return review time into one account. Not only were unrecoverable billable amounts lost until he was set straight, but it also showed that he didn't quite get it.

8. Time summaries also helped us identify considerable time spent on low fixed-fee tax returns because the clients decided to engage in hundreds of day trading transactions or invest in hedge funds with 30-page K-1s that year, which we were then able to partially bill for, and better schedule the following year's tax work.

9. We found that considerable time was spent redoing completed tax returns when amended 1099s were received from the broker. We were able to adjust the timing of the work on those returns in later years.

10. The time run revealed considerable time on extra services such as fixing up erroneous transactions; finding errors in a bank reconciliation and comparing it to the client's checkbook entries; helping a client fill out college loan applications; and sometimes a lot of time was spent listening to a client's ramblings because the staff person didn't want to be discourteous.

11. The time records helped us realize the extra time spent on a small fixed-fee "commodity service" client who would always stop by the office to pick up her payroll and sales tax returns. Since she was in here, she asked if someone could help her by showing her where to sign and who to make out the checks to. Well it seems the person who was usually in the office was a tax partner who would spend 45 minutes to an hour with her also answering other business questions since she was there already. In one year, this unallocated and unscheduled time amounted to 16 hours. We reviewed this with the client and were able to get some extra billing for it (not too much, but more than we would have had if we didn't see this when we did the realization schedule). In addition, since we could not be compensated for this "hand-holding" personalized service going forward that client insisted on, the decision to drop the client was pretty easily made.

12. Client and staff realization can also be charted if you have time records. It helps us with scheduling and maximizing resources by assuring the right level person is working on a client. The realization information also shows us which staff are good at downward delegation, and which managers accept upward delegation from staff. And client fee realization provides the profitability data for each client.

13. Time is our inventory and hours the units. Inventory needs to be controlled. Timesheets seem to be the best way of doing it. If there is something better, then we should look at it. Not having any system or controls is unacceptable and just not good practice.

We all know most of the things that we see in the time records, but looking at the time run forces us to focus in on it in a manner that we don't take the time to do when we are in the middle of getting client work out the door.

45. Raising Rates

Q:

Any suggestions on how I can increase fees?

A.

Any time is a good time is a good time to review your fees and consider increasing them. But the beginning of the year or a new season is especially good.

Keep in mind that whatever the method you choose, you are making a business decision you should handle with care and finesse and can affect the relationship you have been cultivating with the client.

Also, losing the client is always a threat, so you must be prepared for this. Further, not raising the fee also presents a threat to your long-term success and business viability, and this also must be considered.

Seven Ways to Increase Fees

1. Many firms review and increase their hourly rates annually, usually as of January. Some do it more frequently such as every six months, and some never get around to it. The increase may or may not be announced in advance, especially if engagement letters or fee proposals contained wording that fees will be billed at the rates currently in effect when the services are rendered.

2. Some firms that bill fixed fees, retainer fees or value billed periodic fees send letters in December (or earlier) announcing the fees they will bill for the next year. Clients are told that if they have any questions they are welcome to call the accountant to discuss it further. This puts the initiative on the client to call, rather than you calling them.

3. Some firms don't send letters but increase the fixed fees with something similar to the following written at the bottom of the January bill: "Due to increased costs and time charges your monthly retainer has been increased x percent effective January 1, 20XX. "

4. In some instances, clients are called and the increases are discussed over the telephone.

5. In other instances, meetings are arranged to discuss the proposed increases and the reasons for them.

6. Some accountants include with the fee increase notifications or proposals for additional services, add-ons, or special services or upgrades.

7. Many firms use more than one of these methods, depending on the circumstances with each client.

46. What Kind of Expert Do You Want To Be?

Q:

I want to write an article. How do I choose a topic?

A:

If you are young, it really doesn't matter as long as you are published. However, if you are more experienced and want to use the article or speech as a marketing tool, the choice of topic is very important. You want the topic geared to the area of expertise in which you want to present yourself.

An attorney friend who specializes in estate planning recently wrote an article on home office expenses. It was an exceptional article and included many legal citations, but I always thought of him as an estate planner and here he was writing about a tax deduction.

I used to publish a *New Business Kit* with my partners – Peter and Frank. We had six editions and finally stopped. The first couple of editions were exciting and made us authors, the last few were updated by summer interns because it was there and easy to get done. After the initial publication or two, it stopped having any meaning for us – it did drive clients to us, but they weren't the type of clients we wanted. We wanted the person already in a business who was looking to grow, and this book did nothing to attract that type of client.

I do a lot of writing and speaking – I enjoy it and enjoy sharing my experiences with those who care to read and listen. My target is fellow CPAs and not potential clients. I am past the period where I need to bring in new business to survive, and I like to spend some time trying to help other CPAs, which is a sort of payback to those who helped me along the way.

Getting back to my friend, he wrote the article because he could – it was easy, a way to show his rounded ability, perhaps show his clients and prospects he is more than "just an estate planner" and it was a way to be published. However, I think it watered down his image as an estate planner. Anything that diffuses a reputation or expertise in an area is a negative when it comes to getting new business or firming up your ability.

My problem is that I have written so many articles and given so many speeches that it was never easy to identify me as an expert in anything – I like to tell people I am the last of the "expert generalists. "

In this age of specialization and niche expertise, being a generalist is a negative to most people, indicating a lack of competency in their area. I tend to think of the old general practitioner physicians versus the current-day specialists. No one looks at the whole patient.

Well, I was the guy who looked at the whole client and I think this is so about most smaller practitioners and some partners at larger firms. However, when you profess to be an "expert," the image of "knowing everything" is counterproductive to establishing your image.

That being said, what you write and speak on goes a long way toward establishing you as an expert – how you want that expertise to be perceived is your business but you should craft your efforts in that direction.

47.■Advising a Client Buying or Selling a Business

Q:

You have written about an accountant assisting a client selling a business. Is there anything you can tell me about the selling process and how CPAs can be involved?

A:

I love this question. There is plenty I can tell you.

Investment banking is a mystery to many people outside of a small inner circle, with most people only becoming aware of it when they want to buy or sell a business. The CPA's role should be to walk clients through the maze of events that lead to the culmination of the deal, and then to be there afterward to financially ease them into their new situation or status.

A client who wishes to buy or sell any type of business larger than a quite small one will need an investment banker to identify and find the buyer or seller. When representing sellers, their role includes the presentation of the company in its best and most favorable position. When representing buyers, they need to search their inventory for the most appropriate company for them. They also assist in the negotiation process and are a necessary part of the team, just as are the attorney and CPA.

The lawyer is necessary to prepare and/or review the contracts and assist in the negotiations and to put the buyer or seller, as the case may be, in the best legal posture with the most protection.

The CPA is probably the least understood role and yet the most important. (Did you think I would say anything different?) The CPA's role in such deals is actually to represent their clients with the client's own lawyer and investment banker. We say this with complete respect for those other professionals – but we have a unique role.

Accountants most likely have been the closest financial advisers to their clients over an extended period under varying business climates and conditions. CPAs have learned how their clients think, what is important to them and what values they have. I feel that we understand best (as much as any adviser can) what our clients *actually* want out of the deal – not just closing the deal, but why they are doing it in the first place!

It is the CPA's talent and role to help their clients actually decide what they want and to discuss if it is realistic and practical and to chart a course that keeps them and everyone else on the team focused on those goals. Sometimes clients simply want far more than is sensible for a buyer; other times business owners sell themselves and their businesses short and underestimate their real value in the marketplace. This can be done for existing clients, or new ones retaining the CPA specifically for this transaction.

You should start by helping the client articulate his or her thoughts and chart them into an effective course of action. Then the CPA would monitor the negotiations and contracts to see that they are on target with the projections. The CPA is also there to help the client, team and buyer or seller immediately adapt to changing situations.

The CPA's role is also to develop the tax plan that determines the nature of the income if our client is selling or the allocation of the costs (with appropriate appraisals) if their client is buying. Estate tax aspects are also considered as well as the method for insuring the succession of the entity if the client is the buyer.

Additionally, earn out provisions can be constructed, and parameters and safeguards for monitoring the performance if there are any extended payments to the seller.

If the client is the buyer, it is very important to have realistic financial projections with assumptions that are reasonable and that recognize the true situation. The CPA's role is to review the projections or to prepare or assist in their preparation, as the situation warrants. Part of the projections should be to test future compliance with potential bank covenants. The CPA will also lead the financial due diligence team reviewing the financial books and records of the seller.

Where a business plan or offering memorandum has to be prepared, CPAs will work with the client's staff to develop raw data in the financial area, assist in the preparation of projections and help with necessary recasting of the financial statements. We will also see that the investment banker has the materials needed to represent the seller effectively.

48. ■ Practice Management Conferences

Q:

I see that many practice management conferences are always being held. Is it worth the time and money to go to Florida or Las Vegas for two or three days? Will the return be worth the overall investment? I agree that there is always something to be taken from any CPE or conference, but is it really worth it?

A:

I always learn stuff at these conferences – and the more I know of the subject, the more I seem to learn.

I just read a very short management book over the weekend and put one of the ideas into practice this morning – something I always knew, but just wasn't doing, and because of the book, I did it. Should I give "credit" to the book for teaching me something new? I didn't learn something new – but I did something I would not have done were it not for that book. That's what a lot of these courses are for.

I always attended these types of programs and always took away much more than I was ever able to use, but I did use plenty to make it well worthwhile.

Another advantage to these programs is meeting colleagues from all over the country with similar concerns – I found the networking and interactions alone worth the effort and cost of attending.

If you are a sole practitioner without any partner to discuss things with, it can feel isolating. Attending these programs extends your horizons and expands the people you can call with questions.

What I also used to do (and still do) is make note of attendees who ask questions or make comments in a program of an area I want to learn more about and then seek them out to discuss the issues more fully.

On some occasions, I have called people afterward to find out more info from them. This worked particularly well in areas I was not working in, but wanted to get into.

49. Ed, Are You for Real?

Q:

Ed, you seem to cover a lot of areas in these Q&As and other things you write and speak about. Did you really do everything you said you do?

A:

Thanks for asking this question, and you can indulge me a little in my "bragging. " Yes, I did everything I said I did, but I did not do everything that I write about.

Some things are taken from others – either people I speak to, or hear speaking or from books and articles I read and recordings I listen to.

However, I have had a very broad practice over a very long period.

Eight Traits that Made Me a Happy CPA

1. I never turned down business. I did whatever came my way and learned what I needed to get it done.

2. My personal desire for continuous growth and to learn new things.

3. Partners allowing me to do the extras that what I wanted do.

4. Never forgetting that the clients pay my salary and that they must receive value to continue doing so.

5. My eye on the bottom line and end game, which is to accumulate enough to be financially secure at a normal retirement time.

6. Desire to share what I know and my ability to articulate it clearly.

7. A passion for our profession and what I did.

8. Always trying to have fun and create excitement.

A couple take-aways

I can elaborate at length on each of these, but don't want to bore you. For now, I do want to give you a couple of "take-aways. "

Takeaway 1: Don't turn down business.

I get many calls referring business to me and my firm from other CPAs. A lot of this work can be done with little effort by the accountant. When I suggest they do it themselves and that I will guide them in it, they respond they do not want to do it "at this time" because of this reason or that reason – and I then get the work, for which I appreciate the referral.

When I had my practice, I never turned down work, and did whatever it took to get it done. I have many "crazy" stories that can illustrate this, and perhaps this is a project I could put together at a later time.

Takeaway 2: Interact with other CPAs.

In terms of personal growth, none of us knows everything we need to know or should know. Reading, attending conferences and interactions with other CPAs expand your knowledge and allow you to be bolder in trying new things. I've written about this so won't repeat it now, but I am appalled by the lack of reading and attendance at practice management conferences by many of the CPAs who call me with questions.

I am past the point of being upset – it is a systemic issue and not one that I am able to change, except occasionally on a small scale and that is OK with me.

I do my best to help whoever calls me, and that allows me to grow because the questions I get from my colleagues are always interesting and challenging, and they invariably expand my knowledge and experience.

50. ■ The Right Attitude for an Exit Strategy

Q:

I am concerned that I do not have the right staff to take over (buy) my practice when I am ready to retire, or if I want to slow down and work part time. I am 55 and want to work at least eight or nine more years. Do you have any suggestions what I can do now?

A:

I have an unorthodox response. Don't do anything special.

Work the way you want and how you want. When it comes time to set aside your pencil, see what opportunities are available. Probably the best course then will be selling the practice. Here are some specific comments supporting my position.

I believe there is an *inherent conflict* between wanting the best deal when you exit and wanting the best arrangement during the time you are working. Most people generally cannot have both.

Accepting that, the practitioner should then have to decide whether to set up his business in the manner that best fits his personal wishes and work styles, and maximizes their present income, or in a way that potentially maximizes the back-end value.

The trade-off is that you might not get as much for the practice in the back end as you could, or would like to get. Most people are not aware that they are making a choice or that a choice has been made by them by default.

To give you an example, if you were to "build" the practice in a way that maximizes your exit, it would most likely cost you more currently, and inhibit the way you might want to work. For instance, you might need a layer of reviewers or administrators between you and the staff.

With a current strategy, it is you and the staff, or the staff and overhead structure that you are comfortable with. The work would be done quickly, efficiently and sufficiently complete so that your involvement is minimal, but necessary. Your choice of staff would suit your work habits, lifestyle and desire to optimize your current income.

If you let an exit strategy drive the decisions, you might look to acquire staff suitable to buying you out. You might need a more experienced staff, older staff, and perhaps people qualified to become partners at some time, or at a fixed time, in the future.

Instead of having good people at the right positions with the criteria of how well they perform, you would need to evaluate people on how well they can bring in business and handle clients, carry on in your absence, or how able they might be able in the future to make exit payments to you. You would have to spend time evaluating whether they can grow into being a partner, as well as how well they would be able to handle all their eventual responsibilities. Also, in that type of environment, every new person hired would have to be viewed as being something other than you need right now.

Put a price on that. If the extra annual costs for the next 10 years would be $50,000 (or $250,000 or whatever depending upon the size of the practice) to enable you to be properly bought out, it could cost you $500,000. Is that money you could recoup?

Also, there is no guarantee that it would work out. There is a big assumption that the right people are available and just waiting to come to work for you for five to ten years, then want and be able to buy you out when you decide to retire. And what happens if you *have* to retire prematurely? What would happen then? Or suppose they die prematurely? Or suppose you decide you want to continue working indefinitely; would they still be waiting around? Assuming you have the right person or people, wouldn't they be trying to push you into making them a partner and having you commit to an exit time?

Employing an exit strategy in some manner puts a ceiling on the length of time you could work; otherwise, the pot at the end of the rainbow wouldn't be there for the younger people waiting in the wings.

Question: How are you richer? I believe it is by doing nothing.

P. S. If the perfect person comes along, then consider doing something with them. Also, opportunities always pop up when you are in business so keep your eyes open.

51.

Complaining Partners

Q:

I have two partners and they are always complaining that I don't handle enough of the administrative load, but I always feel I am working too hard and don't have any extra time to take over any admin work. Any suggestions?

A:

You told me that one of your partners handles all the bookkeeping, billing and banking, and he seems to be doing a good job at it. The other partner handles all the HR work – hiring, training, and scheduling, and he also does a good job. Both always complain that they spend too much time at it.

You also told me that you have a total staff of seven and all three partners have approximately the same number of chargeable hours – about 1500 a year. Also, each of you seem to be doing the same amount of marketing, which is probably not enough, and you each bring in the same amount of new business each year, but that one of you brings it in from additional services from existing clients not new clients. You all feel you are doing quite well incomewise, so no complaints in that area.

The only friction is that two of the partners feel they are carrying too much of the admin load.

So, why call me? Things look good. Don't upset the applecart. My questioning uncovered a number of issues providing the undercurrent of the problem, but mainly I will deal with the "uneven" admin workload.

It is natural that admin work spread over the partners will not be shared equally.

It should be assumed that the work "floated" up to the partner best able to handle it.

Two of the three partners seem to be handling it fairly well but possibly they don't want to keep doing it and the third partner doesn't seem willing to step in and take it over.

Inasmuch as the income is good and there is no other friction, why not hire an admin person – either full time or part time – to take over some of the workload?

A partner's time is usually much more valuable getting new business or servicing clients than performing admin work. Push the work down. You can hire a part-time person to do the bookkeeping, billing and banking. You can hire a second part-timer to do the HR type of work and other admin work that comes up.

Or, hire one full-time person. But I think it will be easier and less costly to get two part-timers. Many good admin people do not have decent bookkeeping skills and there is no reason to force this when I think there are many bookkeepers looking for a permanent part-time position.

There are always other issues – nothing is perfect. I believe many of the other issues could be resolved by face-to-face discussions at a meeting held out of the office. (I repeat this a lot because many do not do it, and it works great for those that do,)

52. Becoming a Blogger

Q:

I see that you write a blog. Why do you do it, and is this something that I should do?

A:

I write because I like to. The blog posts represent a creative expression for me. I use them to help clients, get business, get quoted, to share some of what I know to hopefully assist others or to offer my opinions on various matters that interest me.

Whether or not it is for you depends on your ability and desire to share what you know, your dedication to writing it on a regular basis and your follow-through to use it to promote yourself or your practice.

Here are some specific benefits and ways to use your blogs.

Writing a blog builds credibility, but not the way you might imagine. Do not expect to post something that will be read by thousands of people who will then call you to become their accountant. When I write a blog, I have a few specific clients in mind (unless it is an ego post that just makes me feel good) and then send it to them.

This establishes my expertise and also answers questions they might have and for which they can act on.

Many clients I consult with are "do-it-yourselfers" and come to me to make sure they are on target, or for some tweaking. These blogs provide them with clear methods to follow should they wish.

I copy and paste particular blogs in emails and send them to reporters and journalists requesting that they consider using me as a source for a future article. It is a long shot for them to search the web and find your blog, but a guaranteed hit when you email it to them this way. I paste it and do not rely on them clicking my link because many won't do that in case it is spam. I do not click links from people I am not expecting it from, so I do not expect others will either.

I now have a body of knowledge mixed into my blog site. Each month I update and provide complete runs of the blogs to those requesting them. I also indicate specific blogs the recipient should look at based on their interests.

I believe it is better to have a blog on a single topic. My partner Frank Boutillette has one on hedge funds, broker-dealers, SEC and FINRA topics and Ray Russolillo has one on charitable giving. They are focused and reach the people interested in those areas, and readers seek them out.

Mine is more general – actually it seems that way and that might make it less sought out. However, there is a direct focus and that is the issues my clients are concerned about – financial planning, investing, estate planning, business valuation, leadership and running a business. It doesn't seem too focused, but my clients read the blogs and call me with questions.

Someone asked me if I cover income taxes and I was surprised when I realized that I haven't blogged anything about taxes (except for the tax rates in effect right now). If you had asked me when I started, I would have said that I would cover taxes a lot. See, surprises do occur.

My partner Tony Nitti blogs almost daily about taxes in a very thorough and humorous way, so I don't think I need to cover what he does. Also, my clients seem more interested in other areas.

And the calls about taxes all go to Peter now, who I also go to for any answers.

156

I am disappointed that my blogs do not generate many comments, and when I get a comment I try to respond to it and hopefully encourage the writer to continue reading and commenting.

Blogging does help set you apart and distinguish you. It is a brand builder. Clients recognize this and the intangible about you goes up a notch.

Staff become aware of the regularity and offer suggestions for blogs. They can even guest write one to get the experience of being "published. " I have found that staff members mention the blogs to clients. And it is an easy way for staff to learn some new things.

I tweet my blogs. I also retweet others in the hope they will repay the favor by retweeting mine. In addition, if someone retweets me, I definitely will retweet them next chance I get. That is "payback. " I also post my blogs on LinkedIn and Facebook. This takes work – about a half-hour a day if I did it right, which I don't.

Writing a blog teaches you to be precise and succinct. When you edit to shorten and tighten it up, you remove excess words, phrases and redundancy. You become a better writer. Francis Bacon said that "Reading maketh a full man; conference a ready man; and writing an exact man. "

Why do anything? Every time I write something, I seem to learn something. That is a personal benefit for me.

You can get started by going to wordpress. com or elsewhere and following their instructions to get a free site. I also suggest you buy and read one of the many books on blogging and social media.

Two books that have helped me are *The New Rules of Marketing and PR, Fourth Edition* by David Meerman Scott and *Social Media Strategies for Professionals and Their Firms* by Michelle Golden. You can also watch the movie *Julie & Julia*, which shows step by step how to run a blog. When that movie's director Nora Ephron died, among her great accomplishments was the credit that she was a blogger. Being a blogger must mean something!

53.■Lowball Fees

Q:

I seem to be getting a lot of new business because I am quoting fees that are much lower than the other quotes the clients are receiving.

However, I don't think I am too low. I am making more money and I am doing some interesting things. But am I doing anything wrong?

A:

This person is a partner in a two-partner firm with two professional staff and an office assistant. When they get special or extra work, each partner does that work. The partners seem to perform equal services, get along great and there are no "partnership" issues.

A few years ago, I had two consecutive meetings – one with an attorney who complained my business valuation fees are too high and the next one, a lunch with two partners from a similar size CPA firm that accused me of "lowballing" fees to get business valuation work. One of the "lowball" fees was for work that attorney was referring to. Fees are very subjective.

I think lowballing is in the eye of the parties to the transaction. Usually fees are quoted at the beginning of an assignment before work actually starts. If the client likes the fee, they accept it and work starts. Usually there is a comparison of proposals from two firms. If there is no perceived difference, the one with the lower fee will get the work. On some basis, all CPAs make a good living. Some more than others, but none seem to be making the huge amounts that might be indicated by continuously "high" fees. If we made that much, many of us would have enough socked away to stop working and do other things where income was not the driving force.

Different firms have different overhead and profit structures. A larger firm will have a layer of people including some experts available to work on a project while a smaller firm might just have an owner who will do all the work by herself. In a smaller firm, there is a direct relationship between doing the work and receiving the payment. In a larger firm, there is a disconnect and in many cases no relationship between the work and payment. The extra revenue is a good driver to try to get as much new business as possible. Also, in many situations there are no added costs to perform services for an extra assignment. QC in a larger firm is more extensive (and possibly assures a better result) and this has to be factored into the costs and fee. In some instances, large firms lowball fees to get an entrance into work they may not presently perform, a client or industry they want to be involved in, or to fill in open time where staff might not be assigned. Fee setting is a very subjective activity.

As to my friend in the smaller firm, his income is much less than counterparts in larger firms and his overhead is lower, so the rates are accordingly lower. Lower rates are not a reflection on the ability to service the client properly. Smaller firms might quote lower for the same service, do the work the same way, and might even make more on that job than a larger firm with higher fees might.

I know of many firms that specialize in a particular industry and were able to make substantial investments in training, systems and procedures to have the work done efficiently and profitably with reasonably low fees in comparison to firms that do not specialize and that do not have the infrastructure for that type of work.

I also know that some of these firms have developed, at considerable cost, a wide expertise with industry experts on their staff so that they have become premier consultants in that industry. To them, an initial engagement of a standardized service, which might be the bread and butter to a typical CPA firm, might be nothing more than a door opener to the more lucrative consulting services. Maybe they don't make as much on the basic work, but they certainly make it on the additional services. That might be lowballing to some when it probably is just a better competitive position. Good for them! Also, I have the feeling they also do quite well on the standardized services.

54. Collecting Old Accounts Receivable

This was prepared for a Q&A column in a business publication and while it pertains to an advertising agency, many of the suggestions also apply to any type of business, including a CPA firm. Further, perhaps you can use these comments to advise clients with these problems. This might also be something controllers can get involved in.

Q:

I run an ad agency and I have some old receivables that I haven't been able to collect. The companies – my ex-customers – are alive and well; viable – they are just stiffing me. Since asking nicely isn't working, I'm interested on your thoughts about how to get as much as I can out of them.

A:

The key here is that the deadbeats are ex-customers. This could indicate dissatisfaction with your services, a decline in their business (which you ruled out) or that they think they could get away with it.

Each of these would require a different approach. Let's look at each one. Also, how you ask can make a difference in being paid.

Dissatisfaction.

Many times customers that are dissatisfied want the vendor to do penance. They don't actually complain, or ask for the mea culpa, but simply don't pay the invoice and await the collection call at which time they sound off – and then pay the bill, or an agreed-upon amount. Ignoring this type of customer usually leads to losing the customer as well as the amount that is owed. The ignoring is probably symptomatic of the relationship where the customer believes they weren't heard or listened to, or given an opportunity to vent. Calling your customer contact directly, not their bookkeeping department, can get this cleared up. This is an unpleasant task, and the longer you wait, the more unpleasant it becomes, but it must be done. Your job is to be paid as much as possible as soon as possible and to accomplish this, you need to call and then keep quiet and listen while the customer rants. A secondary job is to try to get more work from this customer. Settle the bill, get paid and then call to see how you can re-establish the relationship. Assure them that whatever they were upset with will not be repeated.

Alive and well.

Perhaps they aren't so alive and well. Perhaps they put on a big front, and are also stiffing other vendors. Make the same call as above and ask what the problem is and why aren't they paying. I find that companies that are not doing well are supersensitive to suggestions that they are hurting. Even if they are not hurting, such a suggestion impinges on their viability and can put them on the defensive. The goal is to be paid. Another comment is to tell them you will need to turn it over to a collection agent and since there will be a steep commission, you are willing to pass their 33% fee on to them if they make immediate payment. Also, mention that this collection agent typically reports unpaid debts to credit bureaus. If you don't have a collection agent, hire one and find out how they work and their ease or difficulty of reporting the nonpayment to credit bureaus. Caution: Whatever you do, do not lie, and do not put anything in writing without speaking to the collection agent or an attorney. Debtors have specific rights and you should take care not to violate any of them.

Just stiffing you.

Business doesn't work that way. Occasionally there are some nasty people who do business that way, but not everyone who hasn't paid you. Follow the instructions for the other two categories. However, keep in mind that it is impossible to be in business and not get stuck once in a while – it happens. If this is the situation, chalk it up to one of those times. Life's too short to get yourself bent out of shape for these thieves.

Whenever you request payment, make it easy by accepting credit card charges, and suggest that payment be made that way and that they can give you their number over the phone.

Another suggestion is to tell them they can make three equal credit card payments – 1/3 now, 1/3 in a month and 1/3 in two months and you will automatically charge their cards.

Shame on you.

But all in all: Shame on you. Getting paid is essential to running a business. Good practices dictate that you make it clear to your customers that they need to pay you promptly. Establishing this early on in the relationship gets it out of the way, clears the air and becomes part of a normal procedure where you bill and the customer makes payment. I would suggest that for every new customer or client you personally call your contact on the morning of the first day after the payment was due and ask if there is a problem with your services and inquire why your bill wasn't paid, and if it was an oversight, could they please send you a check or provide a credit card to which you can charge the payment. And then stop talking and wait for an answer. Don't speak again until you need to respond to their answer.

I prefer calls to keep the customer on track with payments. No matter the size of your bills, one month's bills cannot be significant to the cash flow of the customer. However, four months of unpaid bills can become significant. Do not let customers fall behind. Service businesses such as ad agencies have payments due for services or media. Most of the media bills are pass-throughs and must be collected as you need to pay the media. This is a quick way to ruin your business and reputation. The service portion of your bill can represent upward of 70 percent payroll costs, which have already been paid by you. Don't be a sap – collect for the work you do.

To help monitor unpaid bills, I suggest getting accounts receivable aging reports at least monthly (with today's software getting this report weekly should not be onerous). These reports should be reviewed by management as received to ensure that invoices appear to be paid within reasonable periods. Also to be reviewed are changes in customer payment patterns, even if the payments are not past due. Be smart! Be diligent! And be alert! Actually, don't be stupid.

55.■Joining
Professional Associations

Q:

I do not belong to my state CPA society and see no value in it. What are the benefits if I am a sole practitioner and just starting out?

A:

I belong to the AICPA, NJSCPA and NYSSCPA. I feel strongly about supporting these societies, and believe it is a responsibility of professionals to do so. I am also active in these three organizations, in different ways and not always at the same time, although I have never been on any of the boards.

The societies offer many benefits just by existing, and many more for those who participate.

Their presence informs the public that there is oversight over the performance, training and validity of the professional designations. They also publish journals, offer continuing education programs, have committees that can provide support to members with questions about issues they are not familiar with and organize member chat and question forums, all permitting the sharing and exchange of information. The societies also look out for any proposed legislation that could affect our practices, and make available membership directories to the public. Active participation is a way to give back to the profession. People sharing help those coming after and offer a form of repayment to those who helped them.

On a more selfish basis, participation enables meeting other professionals with similar practices and concerns, allowing you to discuss problems and not feel alone. Many times practice mergers and sales occur though this participation. There is also committee service, which is an easy way to enable you to share what you know while learning more about areas you are interested in. So too, with giving speeches and writing articles. Other times, it is helpful when you meet people who mention their accountants and when you are able to indicate you know them it elevates you in their eyes. Also you may either get a new client or lose a client and will interact with the other accountant. Knowing them can ease any discomfort and facilitate the exchange of information.

I get many calls from practitioners asking me how they could go about merging or selling their practices, or looking for experienced staff. I am appalled about how many of these callers do not know any other practitioners because they do not participate in any society activities nor do they take advantage of society CPE where they will meet other CPAs because they found "cheaper ways of getting their credits. " (CPE is another area I feel strongly about, but not in this question's response!)

When I consult with business clients that want to sell, one of the first things I ask about is the possibility of their speaking with a competitor who I feel is the most likely purchaser. The same applies to CPAs who call and when they tell me they do not know anyone, I know the price they will end up with just dropped.

We have a license to practice and it is our duty to keep it valuable, and belonging to societies is an important way to accomplish this.

I have many stories about the direct benefits of my participation, and will share one right now. When I had my NYC practice, voluntary peer reviews were new and we did not care to spend the money to get organized enough to subject ourselves to them. When Peter and I formed our firm in 1988 we decided to get peer reviewed as quickly as possible.

We were new and felt that since we were just starting out, we should adopt the most current and best policies and procedures.

About a year after we started, we scheduled a peer review through the AICPA

PCPS Division. We got it done, passed, and that was that. A few months after that we received a letter from a manufacturer saying they were looking for a new CPA and asked us to call if we were interested. We called right away, met with them and got their account. They immediately became our third largest client! I asked them how they got our name and were told that the controller contacted the AICPA for a list of accountants and was sent the PCPS membership directory. They then contacted every firm within a half hour of their office, and we were the first to respond. They liked us, and we got the client. They also had a copy of our peer review report confirming our competency. Membership pays!

56. Pre-Merger Questions

Q:

What do you ask for when considering a merger?

A:

This is a "you show me yours and I'll show you mine. " You should have this information fairly well organized. Also, look at it critically and try to imagine what a prospective partner would say, and how you would react if this were someone else's information that was being presented to you.

25 Essential Data for a Merger or Acquisition Discussion

1. Current partnership agreement

2. Copies of CPA licenses of partners

3. A sample GAAP financial statement

4. A sample OCBOA financial statement

5. Copy of peer review report, any letter of comments and response

6. Copy of malpractice insurance policy

7. Details of any lawsuits during the last five years – either as a plaintiff or defendant

8. Gross revenues for each of last five years

9. Aggregate net income for partners for each of last five years

10. List of 10 largest clients for each of the last two years and the fees billed and collected from them. It is not necessary to show client names

11. Percent of practice relating to specific industries if more than 25% of practice is from a single industry

12. If time records are maintained, number of chargeable hours last year for each partner

13. If time records are not maintained, explain why, and tell how time of partners and staff is controlled

14. Who signs the financial statements

15. Who signs the tax returns

16. The percentage of corporate extensions filed to total corporate returns prepared

17. Ditto for individual returns

18. An inventory listing of special or extra work that hasn't been started yet, or isn't at least 25% complete

19. Dates the five largest financial statements were delivered to clients with fiscal year end of client

20. Turnaround time of financial statements from the review department

21. Ditto for tax returns from tax department reviewers

22. Do any appreciable number (more than 10%) of the tax returns and financial statements bypass the review department?

23. A copy of your staff handbook, or policies regarding overtime and sick pay, and the 401(k) plan

24. A copy or summary of medical insurance plan and what it costs the firm

25. Request to look at a representative sample of work papers used for financial statements they reported on

The above is a listing of things to see. This doesn't replace negotiations, visiting the office, "kicking the tires," getting a feel for the prospective partners and sound judgment.

57 ∎ Partner Out Sick

Q:

My partner has been out sick for the past 3½ months, and he has been continuing to get his draw. It looks like he will be out for some time more, but not sure how long. He does make some calls from home, but isn't really doing any work. Is there anything I can do?

A:

My first question is: Do you have a partnership agreement?

A partnership agreement would cover this, but they don't have one. I started to discuss what would be in an agreement if they had one and perhaps they should deal with this issue accordingly.

How a Partnership Agreement Would Help

I suggest that agreements provide for full draw or salary for three months, and half salary for three months thereafter, and then nothing until they return on the same basis as before the illness or disability. If they continue not to perform for 18 months in a 24-month period, then the buyout provisions are activated. During this period, they will still participate in the profits at their regular percentage. Note that the profits will be higher because of their reduced salary payments, and they will share in that based on their percentage.

That's the easy part. The hard part is telling them. You need to do it. And the sooner the better. If there is a fight or disagreement, deal with it now.

You were both negligent in not executing an agreement and now you need to deal with the unpleasantness arising from this neglect.

By the way, each of the partners should be responsible for obtaining personal disability income policies and these usually kick in after three months. Cutting their draw should not cause your partner undue financial hardship.

A lesson here is to draw up an agreement if you do not have one. And get it done now – it is necessary, important and will make your life better!

58.■Suing a Client

Q:

A former client owes me a lot of money and will not pay or even discuss a settlement. I want to sue him. What can you tell me about this?

A:

I don't know the details so cannot address your specific situation. However, I have some comments about suing that I would like to share with you.

I don't think it make sense to sue clients for fees. Once you sue, you immediately know you will get less because of the costs of the suit, and you are never sure you will prevail. You will also have to spend an inordinate amount of time recreating the situation, invoices and time runs about what the work was for and how it was done and by whom, and have to dredge up old records and dissipating memories. You will waste a lot of time on this plus at meetings with lawyers and depositions. And we all know that depositions are often postponed and drag out – is this what you want to subject yourself to?

Another reason not to sue is that many clients countersue alleging some form of malpractice. And many times, it is for amounts greater than what they beat you out of. This necessitates mounting a defense, further causing you more nonproductive time. It will also put you in the position of possibly defending odd phrases, notations and comments on your work papers that meant nothing at the time. You will need to report the countersuit to your malpractice carrier, subjecting you to their questioning and enquiries, and more added time. Further, some insurance companies will not insure you if you regularly sue for fees.

My advice is to chalk the loss up to your ineptitude in operating your practice and lack of diligence in making sure you are paid for the hard work you did. Leave the past where it belongs – in the past.

59. Billing for Phone Calls

Q:

I have a tax and small business practice and seem to spend a lot of extra time I am not paid for. This includes fielding phone calls about personal issues, financial planning, retirement questions and tax notices. Most of my clients are on fixed or predetermined fees and don't have room for extras. How can I get paid for some of this work?

A:

If a client calls one or two times in a year, I think you have to eat it. If they call more often, or require lengthy responses or if you need to research their questions, then I suggest you bill them.

Here are a number of ways you can do this...

Five Ways to Bill for Phone Calls

1. When you bill them for their next tax return add something extra and label it something like this: financial planning services during the year $xxx. xx. You should charge them a minimum of one hour at your billable rate and in half-hour increments thereafter. If the client asks about it, tell them it was for the calls they made to you during the year and you charged them for an hour (or hour and a half – whatever it was).

2. If they are a business client, add the services to a final year-end bill, or final bill sent in December for "financial planning services during the year $xxx. xx. "

3. Bill immediately after the service is performed for either the time at your hourly rate or the value of the service, whatever you think is appropriate. If they call and ask about it probably acting surprised, simply tell them it is for the work you did in such and such matter and billing them "is how I make my living. "

4. Another alternative after you've had an initial lengthy call on a matter that looks like it will be continuing is to tell the client that there is no charge for this consultation or call, but any time going forward will be billed at your standard rates, based on the value of the services or set a fixed fee.

5. Tax notices are a different issue and you should let a client know upfront whether there will be a charge after you assess the situation. Some firms charge an extra fixed fee when the tax return is billed to cover time spent responding to audit notices, should the client receive one. This is a very common occurrence and a problem area for many firms.

All these methods work – you have nothing to lose by doing one of these things. Try it!

60.

Partnership Buy-Sell Agreement

Q:

I have an accounting practice with three partners. We don't have a partnership buy-sell agreement but we know we need one. We just can't agree on what should be in it. None of us wants to give up any independence, be locked into something or have to start being more accountable. Can you offer some suggestions?

A:

Some simple questions for you…

11 Reasons for a Partnership Agreement

1. What happens if one of you dies suddenly?

2. How will you deal with the your deceased partner's family?

3. How much will you pay them and over what period?

4. Do you think that the family will accept what you offer without seeking advice of an attorney and possibly another accountant?

5. Do you really believe the advisors will tell them to accept your offer without performing some due diligence?

6. Do you realize that due diligence means hiring someone to perform a valuation of your practice?

7. Do you think you will accept the value in that appraisal or will need to hire someone to rebut the report or prepare his or her own valuation?

8. Do you understand what this will cost in dollars and in the lost friendship of your deceased partner's family?

9. Is it possible that one of you will not die, but become permanently disabled?

10. Is it possible that the family will need and depend on cash flow from the sale of their share of the practice?

11. Do you understand that you could be on either end of this situation?

I think it is critical to have a buy-sell agreement to cover death and permanent disability. It is essential to have an agreement that covers every eventuality, but I find that it is much harder to get one when it has been neglected for many years. It also takes much longer.

My suggestion is to get an agreement ASAP to cover only death and permanent disability. You could use my practice continuation letters as a guide (see appendix for this). This agreement will not be binding for any other situation and will not cover important issues such as retirement, withdrawing from the practice, non-compete arrangements, taking clients or staff, who gets to keep the office (or who gets stuck with it!) and who retains the phone number, websites and URLs, partner performance measures and management or administrative responsibilities. These are important and if you are stupid enough not to cover them at least each of you will be around to negotiate or fight it out with each other.

With death and disability, this is not the case and you would be dumping an onerous and terrible situation and process on your family and the surviving partners. Be kind to them and yourself – get the stopgap agreement done and then start work on a permanent all-inclusive agreement.

61 ∎Doing As Little As Possible

Q:

I have many clients who always expect me to do extra work as part of our fixed fee agreement. How can I be paid extra for work beyond the scope of our agreement?

A:

This is a recurring theme, and one that has many answers. Here is another approach.

My friend Brian in Texas has a small practice. He is a sole practitioner with nine employees, and he makes a lot of money. The description he gives of his clients is not impressive nor is his basic operational setup. When he gets a client, he tells them he will do as little as possible and bases the fee on that.

His explanation is that he will only do what they absolutely need and nothing else, explaining that it makes no sense for them to pay for something they don't need, and he fully understands that they need things for compliance purposes that are forced upon them such as income tax returns, payroll or sales tax forms and a possible compilation for the bank.

He goes through their needs, prepares a list with them, determines the frequency of visits or work performance, the deliverable, his availability by phone and an occasional meeting and sets a fee – a pretty low fee –for this work (in his local area there seem to be more accountants than there should be and his fees have to be competitive, which they are), and they both initial the page the list was written on.

Does this sound familiar? It is similar to the value-pricing model of Ron Baker.

Whenever the client calls with a request outside that list, he tells them that this is no longer the "as little as possible" they agreed to, and there would be an extra charge – which he scribbles on a memo sheet and faxes to the client for their initial – Ron Baker's change order!

He usually charges what the service appears to be worth to the client – understanding that he is not competing with anyone else for this work. Every year about 8% of his clients need something extra – whether it is financial information for a college loan application, a financial statement for a bank loan, an asset or cash flow analysis for a divorce, an indication of value for a buy-sell agreement, assistance to a client where a relative died, installation of a QuickBooks® upgrade, a mediation of a fight between partners, a financial plan or asset allocation review, advising on setting up a SEP, SIMPLE or 401(k) plan, a cost accounting or inventory system, or occasional fraud investigation or prevention engagement.

When necessary, he will also do a review report or an audit. He is peer reviewed, has the AICPA ABV accreditation, and amasses about 100 CPE credits a year.

You may have gotten the impression that he is some local yokel because I said he hand-writes a list of services and has the client initial it, or that he faxes his "change orders. " Well, he is one sharp guy. He attends AICPA national conferences, where I first met him two dozen years ago, uses state-of-the-art technology, and belongs to the Boomer Circle and an AICPA national practice group that meets quarterly. But his initial sale is for the minimum that a client needs for a price they are willing to pay.

The takeaway from Brian is that it is absolutely essential to be clear upfront what services you will provide and then be equally clear when there is a crossover into additional services that were not agreed on. Brian's low-key style and method matches that of his clients and their appreciation of him being on their side. He has happy clients, little pressure, satisfied staff, low exposure and a very high income.

A key to being paid for extra work is communication with the client before the work is performed. At that point, it has the most value to the client and the least commitment by you.

By the way, at the AICPA National Forensic & Valuation Services Conference, I attended a session on billing and collections. A common problem is when work exceeds the agreed-upon services. This is so whether there is a fixed fee or time-based fee. It might seem that a time-based fee provides a greater leeway to spend the additional time, but all fees come with a client expectation of the total cost or range, and additional services go beyond that expectation.

A technique that seemed to work was to immediately prepare an additional engagement letter and present it to the client when the need for the new services first came up. For example, when the engagement is for a business valuation and then there's a need for a forecast of the business, so they ask us to prepare it. Well, that is not a two-hour job and a new engagement letter should be immediately prepared. Ditto when working on a valuation for an installment sale to defective trust and an analysis of the cash flow needs to be done because the valuation amount turned out to be much lower or higher than expected.

62.

Outsourced CFO Services

Q:

I have clients that are growing and seem to need more services in-house than they can afford. They are leaning on me provide them. I gather this is an additional engagement . How can I go about it?

A:

It seems that the client is crossing the line into a more sophisticated area, but is not able to afford a full-time CFO. In some cases, these clients have controllers, but they are so overloaded with work they don't have the time to move over to the higher-level services.

These services can include outsourced administrative, bookkeeping, controllership and chief financial officer services. Also, these services can be provided to not-for-profit organizations and governmental agencies and apply to any size organization. CPAs are well suited to perform these services after only a brief introduction to the peculiarities of the organization and its needs. Another type of client needing these services is a well-funded startup. The outsourced accounting relieves the managers from the non-productive work that must be done – they won't become bogged down with what they don't have to do.

Here are some suggestions for your consideration...

22 Guidelines for Outsourced Bookkeeping Services

1. Establish a computerized accounting and bookkeeping system suitable for the business including a chart of accounts.

2. Set up recurring entries and memorized transactions, and configure the program to provide the management information that would best serve client's needs.

3. Set up billing and customer payment system. Bills will be sent directly to outsourced provider for entering into the system. It will then be forwarded to client for payment authorization.

4. Receiving and recording sales receipts. Note: Collection and depositing of sales receipts can be done by client at their office. If so, they will be instructed on the procedures to follow.

5. Generating monthly accounts receivable schedules, if required.

6. Entering the payroll information on client's books from the payroll prepared by the payroll service including recording the tax payments.

7. Reviewing the quarterly payroll tax returns that will be prepared by the payroll service.

8. Bank reconciliations of all accounts with transactions

9. Monthly schedules of accounts payable, if appropriate.

10. Monthly balance sheets and income statements in the form of a trend analysis to be discussed with client via telephone, every month.

11. Review of the annual payroll taxes prepared by the payroll service.

12. Preparing sales and use tax returns (if applicable).

13. Preparation of annual Forms 1096 and 1099 information returns for submission to the taxing authorities and distribution of them to payees.

14. Outsourced provider will properly file all correspondence, invoices, bills and worksheets in a cloud-based secure paperless system always accessible by client.

15. Provide secretarial services as needed.

16. All other bookkeeping services that are considered normal for an endeavor such as clients.

17. Function as a back office to meet front office and management needs.

18. The work will be done on accountant's premises using the latest version of the QuickBooks® Cloud software that can always be reviewed by client anywhere in the world where there is Internet access.

19. Provider will use their personnel and be fully responsible for the work, and the timeliness of performance. Provider anticipates using the same person; however, on occasion they will vary the personnel so client can be assured of sufficiently trained backup personnel, should it be necessary to use someone else. There will be at least two other people in firm familiar with client's system and offices. Provider will be employing personnel trained to work on client's systems and their company on the QuickBooks® software.

20. We anticipate that someone from provider's firm will be working on client's bookkeeping at least weekly. The number of hours will vary based upon the services required.

21. Please note that outsourced bookkeeping services specified in this letter will not include the audit or review of financial statements or accounting services.

22. Please be aware that the outsourced bookkeeping engagement cannot be relied upon to disclose errors, irregularities or illegal acts, including fraud or defalcations that may exist. However, provider will inform you of any material errors or any irregularities or illegal acts that come to their attention , unless they are clearly inconsequential.

32 Guidelines for Outsourced CFO Services

1. Assist in pre-organizational planning including choice of an entity, choice of state of organization and operation, shareholders or members agreements, tax elections, and structuring of equity interests.

2. Prepare all tax registrations and regular filings as well as developing and maintaining tax and compliance calendars.

3. Set up accounting system including billing and receivables, purchases and payables, payroll, cost accounting, activity-based costing, inventory planning and control, budgeting, cash flow and working capital management, analysis and projections, ongoing system needs analysis, software and system product management.

4. Review bank reconciliations.

5. Establish a contact or customer relationship and management system.

6. Arrange for acquisition and financing of communications and office equipment, hardware and digital requirements, and cloud systems.

7. Research real estate occupancy needs.

8. Temporarily invest of excess cash.

9. Establish and monitor credit limits for customers.

10. Establish and oversee delivery of sales reports.

11. Work with management to determine key performance indicators (KPI) and set up a daily or weekly delivery system.

12. Review insurance needs.

13. Risk management.

14. Research employee health insurance coverage.

15. Coordinate with specialists and attorneys employment incentive packages including ISO, NQSO, restricted stock, Section 83b elections, 401(k) and pension plans, signing bonuses and other typical employee benefit plans.

16. Individualized tax planning for principals and key staff.

17. Assist in negotiations with bankers and establishing financing arrangements, and construction of loan covenants and terms.

18. Assist in negotiation with investment bankers and venture capitalists.

19. Provide access to outside advisors with specialized knowledge.

20. Prepare business forecasts, projections, strategic modeling and assistance in articulating long-range plans.

21. Make available multiple disciplines needed in the operation of the organization.

22. Prepare financial statements including notes to financial statements in GAAP, IFRS, OCBOA, FINRA, regulatory agency and other formats.

23. Identificaty special accounting issues and assist with their interpretation.

24. Assist in obtaining and coordinating with independent auditors.

25. Handle SEC Edgar filings.

26. Set up and provide investor communications.

27. Organize annual meetings, staff retreats and sales conferences on and off site.

28. Federal and state income tax preparation.

29. State sales and other tax preparation and filings.

30. Foreign ownership reporting and filing.

31. An immediate turnkey fully functioning CFO level of services is available.

32. Using a CPA firm for outsourced CFO services is having available a firm with the right levels of expertise needed without the ongoing commitment to pay for such services when not actually needed.

63. ■ I Just Lost My Biggest Client

Q:

I just suddenly lost my biggest client. They said they outgrew me. What could I have done to keep them?

A:

Maybe nothing. And at this point, it may not matter, but there are some things you can do to maybe get them back in the future and stop it from happening with another client.

Losing any client is not pleasant, and losing a large client hurts. And when it is sudden, it hurts even more. I will answer this in three parts.

1. How to salvage something from the loss

- Just because you lost the client doesn't mean you can't get them back. The loss was to a larger firm with higher fees. Unless a fixed fee was set, it is likely their time billing will result in sticker shock and an upset client. Further, the client might not be used to low-level or entry-level staff working on their books, further highlighting the close partner contact they had with you. Also, my experience is that the partner from the larger firm will oversee service the first few months, and then back off, preferring their staff to do most of the hand-holding. Most lower-level and many higher-level staff are not able to grasp the importance of the touchy-feely aspect of dealing with a client, and the client will become disillusioned with that, too.

- Be a gentleman about the loss. Tell the client you will cooperate fully with the transition, and then do so.

- Tell the client, in a nice way, that you are not happy about losing them; that you were always fully aware of their needs and growth and figured that when they were ready for a larger firm, you would guide them to one that would be the right fit, but that you do not believe they are at this stage yet.

- Let the client understand that there will be increased costs – not only with the accounting fees, but with additional work the accountants would want done in house by them, and that they might not have the internal staff to get it all done and will need to hire a consultant or outside accountant, like you, to get some of the work done.

- Tell them you are available to help with additional services should they need it and can actually do the individual and business tax returns if they want and that your fees will be lower than the new accountants for this work.

- Larger firms have less of a dedication to getting tax returns done on time. If you never filed extensions or had last-minute rushes for this client, make them aware of that and tell the client to make sure they convey this to the new accountant.

- Keep in touch. Even if they don't ever again use you, they can still be a referral source for you.

2. How to stop it from happening again

• You need to not only be aware of changing circumstances and the client's possible outgrowing you, but you need to speak to the client about it and let them know you have a plan to deal with it when the time comes.

• Let the client know your plan. Explain the growing needs of the client but that it will occur in stages – not all at once. Maybe even prepare a listing of the trigger points. Include a transition to a larger firm you have a relationship with where you can possibly continue in some capacity. They will work that out with you since you've brought them the client.

• Nothing is forever, but the client needs to know that you are keeping up with them with the knowledge and added services, but when their size precludes you from issuing a report or providing a comfort level to the bank, then reality sets in and a larger firm is needed. Tell them you will manage that situation.

• I see this as a "marketing" activity. Just because they are a client and you have a solid, long-term relationship doesn't mean the client shouldn't be reminded of it, and the benefits inuring to the client. Also if your infrastructure is growing or improving so you can provide the needed future services, let the client know. It also doesn't hurt if you are active in the state CPA society and are a presence in the profession, and communicate that too.

• Writing articles, posting a blog or presenting a speech also establishes you as an expert and as a more established "firm" rather than as a sole practitioner or an owner of a local practice.

• If you have partners, let the client get to know them also. If no partners, then let them know who your backup is or who they can contact in an emergency if you are not available. Note: We are accountants – a client's emergency rarely results in a death or disabling action. An IRS agent wanting to close the business or a pair of special agents knocking on the door can be an emergency, but these usually occur during normal business hours and not in the middle of the night.

The point here is for you to be in control and to make the client know and feel it.

3. How to avoid being surprised

- Do not take the relationship for granted.

- Be involved and accessible to the client.

- Not only return phone calls and emails quickly, but initiate them trying to anticipate what is on the client's mind.

- Never lose sight that you are your client's vendor, and while they might give you their undivided attention and share their innermost secrets with you when you are with them, they are always evaluating the value in the relationship. Do not give them reason to doubt the benefits of you being their accountant and trusted advisor.

I have a method to suggest: Assume you receive a letter from the client dropping you. What are the first things that will run through your mind that you feel you should have done, or should have done better?

Do them, or make sure you do them better from now on. That should be your standard in any event, but sometimes standards get relaxed or taken for granted. That's your fault and you shouldn't let it happen.

64. Referral Fee to an Employee

Q:

I got a new client because of one of my employees. Do I *have to* give her anything?

A:

Wrong attitude! You should *want to* give her something. You should be happy that a staff person was able to bring in business.

Many firms offer referral fees, bonuses or commissions. I suggest paying 10% of collections for five years, as long as the employee continues to work for you. Some pay it only for one year, and some indefinitely. Ten percent seems to be a reasonable percent. Some also pay it for the promised period even if the employee no longer works for them. A commission is a commission and it is good business.

I would encourage staff to try to bring in business, and tell them how. It is quite simple. Tell them all they need to do is set up an appointment and you will take care of the rest. You can bring them to the meeting, and you can have them work on the account – that is up to you and there doesn't seem to be a consistent policy for that. It also depends on the type of work and the level of service the client needs.

No matter what it is called, it is added to payroll, is subject to withholding and is reported on the W-2 statement.

When an employee recommends your firm it shows she or he likes working for you and likes what they do. That indicates the right culture – keep it up!

65.■Returning Client

Q:

A client I lost a year ago wants to return. Should I do anything special?

A:

This CPA called me after reading a Q&A about losing a client. She wanted me to know that what I had said works.

She said she had been doing exactly what I wrote and now the client wants to return. The thing that made the difference was a $1,000 bill for a lunch the client had with the new accountant.

There was sticker shock and that was the last straw. The fees were just too high and a lot of her "touchy-feely" availability was missing. Also, while she billed on time, she never charged for lunchtime – which was about twice a year and included sales pitches by her for referrals and additional business from the client.

I told her she should increase her fees about 15%.

All she has to do is increase her rates and maintain a separate rate schedule for that client. She should tell the client that her rates have gone up since they left, and not go into any more details. Her billing rate was over 40% lower than the partners at the larger firm were.

Her overall fees will still be substantially less than the returning client seems to have been willing to pay the larger firm, and her services will be much better and more responsive.

66.

Outsourced CFO Services Fees

Q:

I liked your question about outsourced CFO services, but you did not explain what to charge or how to base your fees. What do you suggest?

A:

I think fees break into different sections:

1. Initial setup

2. Startup period

3. Normalized services

4. Special outside-the-box services

Following is an illustration of the above. This should not be used as actual fees, but as an illustration only. Also, do not use this illustration as a recommendation to use fixed fees, value pricing or time-based fees.

- One time setup for QuickBooks or similar software $1,500

- The first three months the fee will be $90 per hour plus a $400 per month supervisory fee

- After the three-month period we will meet with you and determine together an ongoing fee

- The fee for catch-up accounting and tax preparation will be $3,000

- Special and unanticipated services not included in the fee arrangement will be jointly determined before we commence work

- Before we begin we will need a retainer of $3,000 to be applied to the above services as we perform them

- We will bill you for out-of-pocket disbursements

67.

Introducing Business Clients to Additional Services

Q:

How can I introduce a longstanding fixed-fee client to additional services that will be billed separately?

A:

This is always a sticky point with longtime clients where everything you do has settled into a routine and you regularly do extra work without charging for it. I worked out a method that you can try. Note that there is no harm or detriment in telling a client you can perform services they might need that is beyond the scope of your normal services. I know that this will enhance your standing even when the client declines the additional services.

Any time you introduce this method is an appropriate time to suggest extra work or to line it up for a later time in the year. You do not need to wait to the beginning of a year to introduce the ideas that additional services can be provided. Obviously, you can add any services you want, and delete those that are not applicable or that you do not perform…

Letter to Client

Dear Ms. Client,

This list summarizes the services we will regularly perform for you during the next year (or in addition to the regular services we perform for you).

We also included additional services we believe you should have, but that are not covered by our arrangement and for which you will be billed should you decide you want them.

When we meet, we can review this list so that you are clear on the value of these services and the benefits to you.

Regular Services

- Overview of your QuickBooks® file and suggested journal entries to correct obvious errors
- Monthly trend analysis printout and telephone discussion with you
- Review of internally prepared bank reconciliations once every three months
- Calls as necessary to discuss business activity and any other issues of concern
- Year-end compiled business financial statement
- Year-end coordinated tax planning for the business and owner including individual tax projections
- Annual discussions of applicable employee benefit plans for owner and/or employees
- Yours and your children's individual tax returns
- Business tax returns
- Annual compiled individual net worth statement for discussion purposes and not for distribution
- Annual review of budget with identification of sales volume

needed to cover all expenses, overhead and measurement of profitability or lack thereof as monthly sales exceed or fall below the break-even amount

- If there is an outstanding bank loan, a testing of compliance with covenants

Business Consulting

- Initial meetings for each new item that arises with no limit on the number of initial meetings as long as they are for different issues

Tax Planning

- Discussion of applicability of new tax laws and effective dates

Additional services that can be requested by you:

Business Financial Planning

- Two-hour initial introduction to a business self-assessment using a SWOT analysis for the purpose of starting a process to determine a long-range business strategy
- Two-hour discussion of the value of the business and ways to grow or capture that value and ways it can be dissipated
- Ongoing discussions to assist you in staying on target with your stated long-term strategic plan and goals. Part of our discussions will be directed at the validity and attainability of your strategic plan and goals
- Testing (or installation) of cost accounting system
- Control evaluation
- Risk analysis of your internal bookkeeping and accounting processes
- Review of inventory records management
- Insurance coverage analysis
- Financial Planning

- Written or formal business valuation

Estate planning

- Plans for business continuation or sale in the event of your sudden death or disabling condition OR if two or more partners and they do not have a buy-sell agreement then assistance in preparing a buy-sell agreement OR if you have a buy-sell a review of its continuing applicability
- Individual goal, risk and asset allocation analysis for personal investments

Special Projects

- Tax examination
- Accounting system changes, installation or recommendation
- Sale, merger, acquisition, liquidation or recapitalization type of services
- Bank or loan financing assistance and/or negotiation
- Upgraded Services
- Audited or reviewed financial statements

68.
Responsibility for Brokerage Statements

Q:

I make my clients have their brokerage firms mail me copies of their monthly statements or they give me permission to go online and look when I need to. A client questioned me about something "stupid" he did and wanted to know why I did not warn him about it when I saw it on his statement. What is my responsibility toward this?

A:

I don't know your responsibility because I don't know what arrangement you made with him. However, I do have some comments about this.

When you become involved in something with a client there is the issue of perception vs. reality.

When you have brokerage statements mailed to you or you have regular online access to them, the *perception* is that you review them monthly, or as transactions occur and therefore are "responsible" to report shortcomings, differences, incorrect strategy and possibly fraudulent transactions.

This is exacerbated when there are large market drops and the client wants you to explain why, causing additional calls from the client for something you really have no involvement in.

In some cases, clients transfer large balances to new accounts, and expect you to trace them, even though they did not provide the information for the new account.

In situations where these transfers occurred and you did not ask the client about it for quite a few months, they feel you are "not providing the services you used to that they have become accustomed to. " There also is review and questioning of fees charged by the brokerage or asset management firm.

The above takes time on your part – are you being compensated for it? Just tracking down information for a new brokerage account can take over an hour.

I know a few accountants who had Madoff account statements mailed to them. They were included on the public listing of people with Madoff account losses, causing embarrassment and a barrage of mailings from companies seeking to represent them in efforts to recover their funds.

I don't see any benefit to receiving these statements unless you are being compensated specifically for it and the client knows how much this service is costing them – and then make sure you do a great job tracking everything and informing the client of your findings.

69. ■ Family Tree of Referrals

Q:

I want to clean out my client list of small tax clients because I am just too jammed during tax season, and don't have enough business to hire someone. Should I just drop the lowest paying 10% of my clients?

A:

I never like dropping clients unless you just can't stand them *and* are losing money on them *and* they never referred any new business to you. However, there are times when it is smart to prune your client list.

Many times practices grow where you take every client that comes along. For some that is a good strategy. For others, the strategy could be to accept only the type of clients you feel you could service best and can get the right fees. We are in a personal service business and we make our money by the work we personally do or personally are responsible for and personally supervise. We literally give up or devote part of our lives for the benefit of our clients (and also to make our living). Somehow the living comes – for some a little higher and for others a little lower, but it comes. It is the way we want to spend our time that we need to control.

This starts with a clear assessment of your abilities and what gets you charged up, and where you think you can help clients the most, and for which they are willing to pay your fee based somewhat on the value of what you contribute to them. Regardless of when you started and how much you might have strayed from your original plan, you can always do an up-to-date assessment, and start from that point going forward.

One of the most important ways a practice can grow is for existing clients to recommend new clients. I always valued such referral sources, and this value surpasses the fees I get from them. They look out for me and help me grow – I owe them!

A suggestion is to make a family tree of your clients tracing the referral sources. You might have a small 1040 client refer two other small clients, and one of them refers a mid-size business client whose attorney refers a large client. It all started from that first small 1040 client. Along the way, each branch of that tree makes referrals so the tree grows, as does your practice. Question: Do you look at your small 1040 clients as a bother or favor, or as a future referral source? If you look at them as referral sources, then might I ask you what you are doing to arm them with ammunition to "sell" you?

You should make it a point to make every client aware of the breadth of your services. Talk to them in ways that relate to them, their needs and their capabilities. For instance, if your client works for a manufacturer, let her know that you have an expertise in manufacturers helping them with cost accounting systems, special tax treatment and with acquisitions. If your client has wealthy parents or grandparents, let them know of your qualifications with financial and estate planning. If your client is someone who might eventually want to own a business, then continuously ask him or her about his or her progress and if he or she needs help. Many people start or buy businesses with partners. Try to get involved at the earliest stages with your client and any potential partners. You should never *not* get a client because they used the "other guy's accountant. " Your role is to become the "other guy's accountant. "

Many CPAs are now offering "financial services," which is a dignified way of saying they sell products such as mutual funds, annuities and life insurance. In that case, every client is a potential customer and the tax preparation can be likened to a loss leader.

I never understood how a business could grow by shrinking, i. e. dropping clients. However, if you have a strong strategic plan and equally strong resolve, and your growth is hampered by a bunch of clients that don't fit it, you can bundle them and sell them to someone who would appreciate them. A simple method is to transfer them in exchange for a percentage of collections for a five-year period.

Another reason to drop clients is that they are the type where staff will not see any way to grow professionally servicing those clients. Once again, this has to do with your plan. If you hire out of school and have a rigid training program, the staff could become disillusioned with clients who just churn dollars for the practice and don't offer any professional challenges. Retaining those clients would hamper or hurt your growth. On the other hand, if you use per diem people who are just buying time until their practice grows sufficiently and you can make a profit with those clients then why not keep every client you can?

Also, if your exit strategy is to sell the practice, then possibly the larger volume will get you a higher price. A warning is that a group of bad clients can reduce the image of the practice and lower the multiple you will get.

70.■Target Clients

Q:

I want to start the year growing my practice but I'm having trouble defining my target client. I tend to accept every client I can and seem to have clients all over the place. Is there anything I can do to better target my "ideal" clients?

A:

Sounds a little like the previous question and some of the responses there could apply to this, but I will be more specific here.

To have a target client means you have a target. The target is the result of a plan. So, what is your plan?

Target clients come in many variations. You can target an industry or a service, and both can have subparts. I identified over 35 subspecialties in taxes! An industry specialty can include professional practices, manufacturers, distributors, construction contractors, restaurants, hotels, not-for-profit organizations, local governments, broker-dealers, real estate and technology firms. Service specialties can include taxes, financial planning, bankruptcy, forensic accounting, business valuations, audits, and budgeting, forecasts and projections.

After you've identified your specialties, you need to establish your expertise and reputation. This comes from writing articles and blogs, being quoted, presenting speeches, joining trade and industry organizations, attending meetings, becoming active in committees and meeting influencers who can refer business to you.

To hone your skills you will need to take courses, attend specialized CPE and read trade journals.

You need to communicate your expertise, which takes special skills, and you should consider hiring marketing consultants to assist you. Note: Occasionally I notice an ad or strategic placement of an interview of an accounting firm I know of that is quite impressive. When I speak with the managing partner and ask how they came up with the idea or concept, they tell me, without exception, that they hired a marketing consultant – that process works for those that are serious about growth.

You also need to assess your capabilities to handle business and offer the full range of services expected in that specialty.

I know many accountants who decided to specialize who have become quite successful. However, they all told me that it takes quite a while, measured in years, to develop the client and referral source base where they did not have to take on other business. Also, merging or joining a larger firm where their client base could jump-start your growth into that specialty could be a consideration.

71. When a Client Threatens to Sue

Q:

A former client wrote me a letter threatening to sue me for bad services. I did nothing wrong, actually did a great job and they still owe me money. What should I do?

A:

Walk away! Ignore the threat. Don't respond. Stop billing them. And go about your business. Life is too short to get tied up in dissipating actions. It is rare to run a business without getting stuck by someone.

If you are sued, you will have to notify your malpractice insurance carrier and it will likely cost you the deductible. If you sue for a fee, you can almost count on a countersuit for high multiples of what you are suing for, also costing you the deductible.

A little more salt on your wound is when the deadbeat asks or demands you send copies of his returns to his new accountant. Do it graciously without comment, and be glad you don't have to deal with that cow-dowdy head anymore.

Would you believe I got three calls on this last month?

72.∎Buy-In

Q:

How can I get buy-in in the implementation of new things we decide to do?

A:

I find buy-in the key to a successful program. It is also extremely hard to get. It is easy in the boardroom or at the meeting when the new process or procedure is agreed to, but then there has to be a champion to be responsible for the follow-through and success.

My suggestion for buy-in effectiveness is for the leader or project champion, e. g. CEO, owner, team leader, to develop a vision and plan to achieve it, explain it with the end result and how it will affect everyone at the company, chart the details, and obsessively go forward with it.

Buy-in is probably the hardest part of introducing change since not every partner is on the same page or is willing to change what they individually do, even if they agree on the benefits and use of the new procedures for everyone else in the firm.

Two good books on change are

- *Who Killed Change?: Solving the Mystery of Leading People Through Change* by Ken Blanchard, John Britt, Judd Hoekstra and Pat Zigarmi and
- *Our Iceberg is Melting: Changing and Succeeding Under Any Conditions* by John Kotter, Holger Rathgeber, Peter Mueller and Spenser Johnson.

17 Ingredients for Successful Change Management Projects

1. You need complete buy-in by all levels of leadership team and management

2. A beginning statement by the "boss" with reasons for the change, input going into the decision-making process to adopt the change, a plan on how it will be achieved, details of the execution, and desired end result and benefit to everyone

3. Company culture needs to embrace change

4. Leadership commitment

5. Sponsorship and guidance

6. Cohesive change leadership team

7. Effective communications and dialogue

8. A sense of urgency

9. An inspired vision that is clearly transmitted

10. A wide-range plan

11. Detailed plan of accomplishment

12. Realistic budget applied with discretion

13. Adequate, full and fun training

14. Achievable incentive plan

15. Timely performance measurement

16. Documented activities

17. Accountability by each team and each team member

– Based on *Who Killed Change?: Solving the Mystery of Leading People Through Change* by Ken Blanchard, John Britt, Judd Hoekstra and Pat Zigarmi. © 2009 by Polvera Publishing and John Britt. Published by HarperCollins.

73. Out-of-Sync Partner

Q:

My partner seems to always be out of sync with me, but my biggest pet peeve is that he never does what he says he will do. Do you have any suggestions?

A:

Some people are not cut out to be partners. They could be control freaks, someone who skipped kindergarten and didn't learn to share, dogmatists who always think they are right, someone who doesn't like to compromise, someone who runs on his own clock, people who don't feel they should have to account to anyone for their time or what they do, people who don't like to or know how to delegate, those who do not understand the value of a collaboration, or you have a partner who is a "character."

I am sure there are also many other reasons, but you can get the idea from these. It is also possible that a partner is embarrassed about a specific issue and wants to avoid doing it. However, this question is about repeated noncompliance and not a once-in-a-while deviation.

If you have a partner like this, or if you are like this, then you need to extricate yourself from the situation.

However, if you are in that circumstance, let's see how you can make the best of it or try to correct it. Here goes...

11 Tips for Staying in Sync

1. You have to speak to them the first time something is not done or followed through on.

2. Ask them the reason, trying to find out whether they agree with what they already said they would do. It is possible they changed their mind, or never agreed with it, but said they did to get the meeting or "confrontation" over with.

3. You need to do this even though this has previously been jointly decided upon.

4. If necessary, decide on something else or a different way so that they can commit to following through on their share of the project.

5. It is possible you and they did not agree to the same thing. Find out what they agreed to.

6. The earlier you have the accountability discussion the better the chance you have of getting back on track.

7. If the aberration is not quickly called to account, then the project is abandoned by that partner.

8. There is nothing wrong with having the project canceled or changed, but there must be communication between the partners to that effect.

9. It may be that a different partner is better suited to that task. If so, make that arrangement and don't saddle a partner with something they are not good at.

10. Having regular partner meetings – for larger firms once a month and smaller firms twice a month – can keep people on track. I noticed that many people who are assigned tasks do not do them until they *have* to do them. Follow-up meetings create the deadlines and add urgency. You can compare this to a volunteer committee where action items are designated and most of the items are done just before the next meeting. The successful committees have more frequent meetings than the failed committee projects.

11. Have an annual offsite retreat. I've previously written on the benefits of this. The retreats can bring up big-picture issues including the repeated failure to follow through.

If you ever wondered what a managing partner does, this is one of the things – keeping the partners on track to do what they said they would do.

74.Value Pricing

Q:

I have a small practice and always charge by the hour and clients agree to it because my rates are not that high. However, with more and more frequency, I find that clients are arguing about the time spent and want either a complete accounting or discounts. Is this happening to other firms?

A:

First, what is happening at other firms should not be your concern. You have your own practice with your own costs and rate structure and what you need to make has to come from the way you price your services. Obviously, there is some competitive pressure, but that doesn't seem to be your issue. Your clients engaged you at your rates and seem to feel you can do the job for them.

I think your problem is threefold.

1. One is that the client is either not aware of the scope of the project or does not have an idea or range of the total cost.

2. The second is that your time spent does not relate to the value the client received, so they are unhappy with the amount. You told me your rates are relatively low, but you didn't say how fast or slow you usually work. You also told me that in some situations you shave the time a little since you feel some of the time was not

productive.

3. Clients and small clients in particular, usually never buy time. They buy a project result or the solving of a problem. So it seems you are selling something different from what they want.

I have a couple of suggestions.

If you want to keep pricing your services by the hour, then I think it is necessary to quote a range or upper limit. Then not only will there be no sticker shock, but the client will have an understanding of what the cost will be of what they want. Note that in some types of engagements you have to be crazy to quote a ceiling – these are where the work is open ended and you have no idea of what you will find or become involved in. Examples are forensic investigations in a marital dissolution or a bankruptcy, or a fraud where what is known could be the tip of an iceberg.

Eight Elements in Determining a Value-based Price

A better suggestion is to quote a fixed fee based on

1. how much time you think the project will take,

2. the perceived value to the client,

3. the complexity of the issue,

4. the size of the transaction,

5. the availability of other CPAs to perform these services,

6. time constraints,

7. assumed support and cooperation by the client and

8. possibly the pain you will be removing from the client.

This then becomes a value-pricing situation, which I feel most accounting services should be.

I have a few problems with time billing.

1. Actually, once you provide a range, you are setting a value price even though you may not realize it. If that is the case, why not remove

the hours from consideration and just quote a fixed fee? If the client at that point thinks it is too high, you can explain why it is a great bargain, or you can negotiate a fee acceptable to both of you. You are in a much stronger position before you do any work, than afterwards. You can also now determine payment terms and ask for a partial amount up front.

2. The second issue is that when clients see the hours, they find it hard to relate to the value, especially if some of the time seems to be nonproductive to their project. It also gives them something to argue about to reduce the fee. As a professional, it seems somewhat demeaning to have to account for time on an hour-by-hour basis especially when value was delivered. Eliminating the time bill eliminates this issue.

3. The third issue is that clients might not feel the value as much when the job is completed as before it starts. One way to look at this is for a client who has not filed tax returns for six years and the IRS is on their back. The value at the point when they rush into your office with six shopping bags of receipts is much greater than when they receive the six completed tax returns in a neat little package. Price the value, not the hours.

I am a big fan of value-pricing guru Ron Baker and although I do not agree with everything he says, I find it incredible that many CPAs have not read any of his books or understand his methodology.

Anyone in a professional services business must read his material and consider and absorb his ideas. I've mentioned this before and am repeating it here. Read his book *Implementing Value Pricing* by Ron Baker (Wiley 2010) and also read *Bill What You're Worth* by Dave Cottle (AICPA 2011). They both have other books and I believe I read them all and they are all good. These are their most recent books.

75. Preparing for a Meeting

Q:

Two clients asked me to assist them in negotiating an important contract on their behalf.

The first client's "adversary" self-published his business autobiography and I decided to read it before meeting him so I would be better prepared to deal with him. It took me five hours to read the book. The second client's "adversary" was a private company and I had my firm's forensic research team gather some information about that company. This took them three hours and out-of-pocket costs were $175.

I have no issue with charging for the latter research, but should I charge the full time for reading the book?

A:

This is along the line of value pricing.

To answer your question, I would charge for reading the book. It was purely to assist you in the negotiation and not for your general knowledge or enjoyment, although I am sure you got both as well.

Your question raises the issue of when value pricing is applicable. Ron Baker will contend it is applicable in every situation. And on some level, maybe so since every fee the client receives is a value fee – the client assesses whether they received value for the amount charged.

The difference in Ron Baker's model is that the value is determined jointly before the work starts. Otherwise, the client does it unilaterally after the work is completed.

Negotiating on a client's behalf would call for the greatest skill level the CPA has, and naturally should be priced accordingly. Assuming it is a big-ticket issue, charging by the hour seems to reduce the value added into a series of tenth of hour units where a slight deviation from conventional time clock punching raises an issue – such as reading a book by the adversary.

Further, how is the time charged for thinking out the strategy while you are driving your car or watching television news? Would . 3 hour be the correct timesheet entry? I would think that a fixed minimum fee for the project would be better for such engagements, along with a right to negotiate a bonus with the client based on results; let the client determine the proper additional fee or a predetermined bonus based on results.

In many situations, a bonus might not be applicable, such as where the negotiation is with a key employee to discuss their long-term incentive package, or to help unwind a partnership. But there is a value for your involvement, and it certainly has to be more than the "tenths of hours" you spend. In these situations, I feel it is more appropriate to charge a project fee that you and the client agree on. Every project engagement should have specifics of what is to be done or accomplished and a time limit. It should not be left open-ended.

What you bring to the table when engaged for a specialized activity is not the hours you will be spending, but the lifetime it took you to acquire the experience to be able to show up at the table.

Also, in the old cowboy movies, I never saw the bounty hunter being paid by the bullet.

76.■I Just Lost a Good Staff Person

Q:

Two calls with same question: "I just lost a good staff person. " One left to go into private, the other went to a larger firm. What could have been done? Or what was done wrong?

A:

For starters, unless you have the size firm where a staff person can become a partner, you have to assume that everybody will eventually leave. No one will be with you forever. And if you do elevate staff to partner, that is always a long shot based on the number of people who start versus how many eventually become partners. So the issue is how to keep staff as long as possible and not to lose too much value when they leave. No, I am not a cynic, I am being realistic! "Reality is not what you want it to be, it is what it is. " I believe this quote is attributed to Jack Welch.

- Reality: Staff will leave.
- Reality: You will lose value when they leave.
- Reality: You might be glad that that person left.
- Reality: You may have caused the person to leave sooner than they wanted to.
- Reality: Everything you do creates impressions that cause staff to

stay or leave.

- Reality: You transmit feelings about your firm to the families of your staff and they become stealth supporters or detractors.
- Reality: There are some easy things you could have done to delay the inevitable.
- Reality: Sometimes they leave for really stupid reasons that they quickly regret.
- Reality: You need to replace the person that left. By not acting and taking charge when someone needs to be let go, they choose the time they leave and when you need to replace them, not you. Usually this occurs at a worse time for you.
- Reality: You run a business and this is one of the things you need to deal with – just hope that it isn't too often and multiple people quitting aren't bunched together.
- Reality: Public accounting isn't for everyone.
- Reality: I am not avoiding a response – I am just setting the scene.

For starters, just because staff people will leave is no excuse to not train them fully and teach them as much as you can, or expose them completely to your clients. As long as they are working for you, they should be given every opportunity to do the best job they could do and to relieve you of as much work as they can. The more they do, they better your practice, and leverage, will be. The trick is to train staff with a degree of uniformity so that when they leave the work they do can be easily replaced, and for you to maintain your relationships with your clients, so there is no threat of losing the client.

I view someone leaving to go into private as a loss for our profession. The person leaving attended college and an extra year thereafter with the goal of becoming a CPA and working in a CPA firm. I believe that the Big Four hire 70% of the accounting majors and 90% of them leave those firms and the profession after three years. That means that the Big Four destroy the desire of 63% of the accounting majors to remain with CPA firms. Terrible!

Smaller firms, which include 96 of the Top 100 firms as well as every other of the 35,000 firms, only have a crack at 30% of the accounting majors. Within that group, the people with the highest percentage remaining in the profession are those who work at the smaller firms. With this in mind, it is important to retain staff and keep them in the profession as long as possible. A message here is that the larger the firm the graduate starts with, the lower the retention in the profession. That reduces the pool of experienced people to draw from to replace someone who left.

Back to your firm. Some things can be done to increase retention…

19 Easy Staff Retention Ideas

1. Better hours during tax season,

2. a continuous "selling" of the benefits of tax season for staff (I have a list – email me for it),

3. making sure staff are presented work they will enjoy and find stimulating,

4. setting up self-checking methods so less work is submitted that needs to be corrected,

5. a "floating" weekend day off during tax season,

6. close the office the weekend after March 15 and the day after April 15,

7. sending flowers or plants to the spouse of a staff person,

8. dinner on you after tax season,

9. a surprise gift for young children of staff,

10. no Mickey Mouse overtime payments – pay for the work,

11. don't make people work late before there are actual tax returns to do, better scheduling of work,

12. occasional surprise ice cream or yogurt treats in the afternoon,

13. St. Patrick's Day beer fest at the local bar and no work that night, and many other things that will interest, excite and provide some fun.

Other things to excite that are not during tax season can include:

14. a day at a ball game,

15. family picnic,

16. tailor-made level-appropriate CPE,

17. unusual CPE such as a comedian economist (they do exist and I have seen a couple),

18. a CPE program at Atlantic City (or similar resort) the first Thursday and Friday in May after tax season ends (with a CPE program from 1 to 5 on Thursday and 8 to noon on Friday) and give

the staff money for dinner and entertainment so they don't have to spend the entire night with you (no matter how exciting you think you are, you are a generation older than your staff and they want to have fun with people their own ages),

19. or a trip to a museum followed by dinner and a Broadway show. (Note, we have done all of these).

Many firms recruit carefully and diligently and then forget about the after-sale marketing – you need to continuously excite your staff.

You also need to have the staff grow professionally – you need a mix of work, expansion of their abilities, continuous training, continuous learning by them, and put them on some exciting clients. An exciting client is defined by me as a client you do exciting work for – not a client who is in an exciting business, although that also helps. And you need to let the staff person know that they are doing exciting things, are learning and are growing – you cannot and should not assume they know it. Sell, sell, sell!

Doing the right things will help you retain staff and also keep them in the profession should they leave you.

Also, pay well. $5,000 extra salary for a staff person means a lot less to you than it will mean to them – and extended retention will have you paid back in multiples.

If the average stay at a firm is three years and it is stretched to four years that is a 33% greater retention. If a two-year average becomes three years, that is 50% greater retention. If six years becomes seven years – well you get the idea.

77.■How to Nurture a Staffer's Professional Growth

Q:

After I wrote about staff retention, I received a call from Michael Slotopolsky of Vision Financial Group telling me what he is doing to retain and excite staff.

He laid out a plan for how a staff person could grow, and he said I could share it with you.

A:

I put it in checklist format.

Staff Development and Growth Checklist

This is a guide to assist staff in their development and for them to understand some of what is expected.

> 1. Be up to speed in learning the new tax laws that will affect the tax returns you will be working on. This is for individual as well as the

entities you will be working on – 1065, 1120S, 1120 and 990.

2. You will be judged on the quantity and type of review notes the reviewers make on returns you worked on.

3. Keep your work papers orderly and make sure they can be easily followed.

4. Diligently manage your workload and client responsibilities, and your follow-up to receive missing information.

5. You should always be on time for meetings and meeting your commitments.

6. You need to fit in with our culture, be an effective team member, and be an enthusiastic firm and profession advocate.

7. You are responsible for following all of our procedures.

8. You will be evaluated by your success with supervising and training staff under you, and your ability to report problems and assess the staff. Note that we are always available to assist you in this and any other area you feel you need guidance in – we are here to help you succeed.

9. You are expected to be familiar with the topics of the articles, and content relating to areas you work in, in all the journals you subscribe to and for this to be done timely. It will be assumed by us that this is done by you within a week of your receipt of the journals. Note that we will pay for any journals you want to subscribe to. At a minimum, you should read the business section of a major daily newspaper, or the *Wall Street Journal.*

10. Besides taxes, you will be working on audits, reviews and compilations. Your attention to the instructions, response to the training and progress will be evaluated by your supervisors and us.

11. Before you start any assignment, you should review the audit, review or compilation programs and procedures, checklists and the prior year's financial statements including the notes. Also, review some public company financial statements that are in the same industry, if possible.

12. You should try to obtain an understanding of the client's business so you will have a running start when you enter the client's premises. This can include looking at the client's sales literature and website. If you work on something in the office, you should still obtain an understanding of the client's business and what they do.

13. You will be evaluated on your assumption of responsibility for regular work on some small clients. This will be overseen by us, but you will need to "push" us in this regard should it not occur to your satisfaction.

14. We always welcome new ideas and suggestions from staff . Be free with your comments and ideas, and do not worry that they might seem naïve – sometimes naïve comments indicate a need for clearer instructions or lead to big ideas.

15. You will be provided with an evaluation after you complete an assignment, and will be given a formal performance and growth evaluation at six-month intervals. Each of these should have input from you as well as us.

78.■Conflict Checks

Q:

One of my partners got a new client (the wife) in a divorce situation that I did not know about.

It turns out that I was informally advising the husband who was a friend of mine and he put me down as his advisor (without my knowing about it). When my partner and I compared notes, we had to drop the client. How can this be avoided?

A:

There are a number of issues here.

Six Touchy Issues When Clients Divorce

1. You have to be aware that any advice you provide to someone in a divorce or potential litigation matter can have you designated as an advisor and possibly have you as a witness, and that you won't have privilege.

Occasionally you might prepare a short memo or calculation and find out a year later that it was submitted and you need to be deposed as an "expert. " Scary stuff.

My advice is not to offer any advice and certainly never put anything in writing – even a seemingly harmless email – without being clear what the issues are and being formally retained. This may make it hard to refuse a friend with some "friendly" advice, but then you won't end up as a witness against the other spouse who is equally a friend to you.

2. Any advice you offer without a full understanding of the situation will usually be incomplete and possibly inaccurate, while the client will think it is complete and fully applicable to their situation. As time goes on, your informal friendly advice will become dogma to the client.

3. In litigation it is important in many cases to be retained by the attorney so you will have privilege. This is particularly so in criminal matters.

4. In many situations, such as in an estate controversy, there are many parties, some with authority to retain you on behalf of the estate, executors, trustees or guardians, and some with no power as they are people contesting the will, trust or court ruling. It is important to know the players, their authority and all the issues.

5. You should never accept a client in any conflict without doing a conflict check with your partners or others in your firm who may have a relationship with one of the parties. Based on the size of your firm you might also include senior managers and retired partners who still maintain an office. In my firm, this is routine. The conflict checks should include the plaintiff and defendant, their attorneys and any experts you are aware of.

6. Carefully review the conflict checks to see who the attorneys are. Some are really bad people to deal with and in those cases, I like to share (verbally – never by email) my feelings and reasons with my partners before they get involved in a situation that might be fraught with danger – at best.

79. ■Time Management for Partners

Q:

I never seem to have enough time to get my work done. The interruptions are nonstop and my workload seems to continuously mount up. Any suggestions?

A:

What does a partner do? What should a partner do? How does a partner *learn* to be a partner? Following is a discussion of what partners do, or should do and a sample listing of how they spend their time.

1. Role of the partner

On some level a partner functions variously as a CEO, COO, CFO, CMO, CIO, chief technical officer, head of QC and even picks up paper clips, or turns off calculators staff leave on. A partner is the owner and boss and everything is his responsibility. In larger firms, there is a division of some of these functions, but even non-managing partners have administrative work – preparing timesheets, bills, staff scheduling, ordering or requesting supplies, deciding whether to close early the day before a holiday, fixing things that break or figuring out that they can't do it and calling someone who can, and many other things that need to be done in an office.

2. How a partner spends his or her time

The preceding table approximates how most partners spend, think they spend, want to spend or should spend their time.

This assumes a 10-hour day and a 45-week work year. It does not factor in tax or busy season or evening marketing meetings. But the 10-hour days, on average, seem reasonable as do 1,400 chargeable hours.

Of course there are differences between large and small firms and those with specific administrative or managerial functions, but this presents a schedule to get you focusing in on what you do on a regular basis.

I've spoken to a CPA firm partner with 2,800 total hours, one with 2,000 chargeable hours, as well as one with 800 chargeable hours, with all three complaining to me they don't seem to be able to get all their work done, and feel they are working too hard. In those three cases, it seems they are each doing either administrative work they could pass on to an additional admin employee, or doing a much lower level accounting work, but don't want to spend the money or spend the time showing a new employee what to do! This chart is a guide to get you thinking. Use it as such.

3. Types of interruptions

Many partners complain of interruptions. Nowadays there are continuous disruptions in our routine and work time. The best way to handle this is to block out "quiet" time. That is when you close your door, keep your phone in your briefcase and not answer the phone, open emails or accept interruptions. If you feel the need to look at every new email, answer every phone that rings or let people walk in at will any time at all, then it is your fault – yell at yourself or set up a new routine.

Some of the more common types of interruptions are:

- People who have general comments, want to chat, let off steam, want to know where they could find something or who have a "simple" question that they would have worked out if you weren't in the office then and there
- Someone who needs you to do something (that just came up) quickly (it may only take only 15 minutes or so) who probably was too lazy to do themselves

How Partners Spend Their Time

	Chargeable %	Hours worked			Hours chargeable		
		Hours/ Day	Hours/ Week	Hours/ Year	Day	Week	Year
Telephone	75%	1. 3	6. 3	281. 3	0. 9	4. 7	210. 9
Email	50%	1. 0	5. 0	225. 0	0. 5	2. 5	112. 5
Postal mail		0. 2	1. 0	45. 0			
Social media		0. 3	1. 3	56. 3			
New work	100%	1. 00	5. 0	225. 0	1. 0	5. 00	225. 0
Regular work	100%	1. 3	6. 0	303. 7	1. 3	6. 75	303. 7
Reviewing	100%	1. 0	5. 00	225. 0	1. 0	5. 00	225. 0
Meet w/staff	25%	0. 5	2.	112. 5	0. 1	0. 6	28. 1
Meet w/client	100%	1. 3	6. 5	292. 5	1. 3	6. 5	292. 5
Proposals		0. 2	1. 0	45. 0			
Marketing meeting		0. 3	1. 5	67. 5			
Product dev't		0. 1	0. 5	22. 5			

How Partners Spend Their Time

	Chargeable %	Hours worked			Hours chargeable		
		Hours/ Day	Hours/ Week	Hours/ Year	Day	Week	Year
CPE		0.2	1.0	45.0			
Read journals		0.2	1.0	45.0			
Personal dev't		0.1	0.5	22.5			
Write, speak		0.2	0.7	33.7			
"Walking around" time		0.5	2.5	112.5			
Administrative		0.4	2.0	90.0			
Total		10.0	50.0	2,250	6.2	31.1	1,398
Hours Chargeable		6.2	31.1	1,398			
Percent Chargeable	62%						

- A partner reminds a staff person (or a staff person reminds a partner) to do something
- A partner asks a staff person to do something so we get it off our mind (aren't we interrupting someone and causing them to lose their train of thought?)
- We don't want to lose track of something and want an immediate answer
- We need additional info – suppose there are two or three such things a day?
- A "how to" that might require two or three phone calls and may happen two or three times a day

A decision needs to be made – why at that moment? Why wasn't it scheduled? Why does it have to be made by a partner? What is the amount of time lost if a wrong decision were made?

4. The partner's role encompasses everything that can be done in an accounting firm, plus all the technical and professional skills needed to service clients, plus the networking and marketing to maintain a flow of new business opportunities, and the interpersonal skills needed to articulate and communicate ideas to clients.

A *Wall Street Journal* story about how a CEO spends his time isn't much different from what I wrote above about the "average" CPA firm partner. The article referenced a study of CEO time 40 years ago, brought it up to date and concluded that there hasn't seemed to be much change in the way CEOs spend their time over that period. The bottom line was that CEOs spent most of their time in some sort of face-to-face interaction, with continuous interruptions and rarely more than 15 minutes without a distraction.

The article pointed out that the "personal interactions are critical to learning the information necessary to run a company effectively. "

The percentages of time blocks are shown below. What is not known is the number of hours a day they work.

- Working alone: 13%
- Calls: 6%
- Email: 7%
- Public events: 2%

- Business meals: 5%
- Meetings: 67%
- Total: 100%

– Managerial Capital at the Top: Evidence from the Time Use of CEOs, by Oriana Bandera, Andrea Prat and Raffaella Sadun, Harvard Business School (2012)

80. ■ Type of Office and Car

Q:

What do you think is the impact on a small CPA firm regarding:

- The town the office is located?
- The physical aspects of the building's exterior and interior?
- The appearance of the firm's actual office space?
- The type of car a partner drives?

A:

I don't know if you'll believe this, but as soon as I responded to this question, I got another call with almost the exact same question. One CPA was in New Jersey and other in Florida.

I don't think the town where the office is matters as long as the accountant is active in that local community, and is accessible to his clients. I think there is a difference if someone is starting a new practice or moving the office of an established practice. When starting a new practice I think it is better to have the office in the town you live in. You can become active in the community and be a presence, which indicates availability. If you are married and have children, participating in the children's activities as a coach or on committees or groups they participate in will spread your reach. Also, your spouse will create a presence for you even by quietly contributing. Belonging to a church, synagogue, mosque or temple also expands your circle of acquaintances. I don't think it is necessary to be pushy or an in-your-face type of person. Being there, joining committees and getting a reputation as someone doing their share of work such as envelope stuffing and phone calls creates the image of a serious businessperson and a trusted advisor.

I think it is important what community you live in. Living in an upscale area will make it easy to meet a higher level of potential clients than if you live in a less affluent neighborhood. However, I don't recommend getting in over your head and buying a house for more than you could afford. Also, it is not just the cost of the house and mortgage, but higher taxes and insurance, greater church contributions and other living costs.

Having an office in a different town than where you live might create a better image, but you won't meet local people.

If you move your office to a different town, clients accustomed to coming to your office might find it difficult and you can lose some business that way, unless you maintain desk space, a conference room or meeting facility to service these clients. I don't think it will matter at all for business clients where you typically go to their office.

The building your office is in should be reasonably well maintained on the exterior and interior. It should not look dangerous, grungy, or unmaintained. Your office should have a nice and comfortable waiting area and conference room. If you usually meet with clients in your office, then it should reflect your personality, interests, and professionalism, and should not look messy or that you are not in control of what you are doing. People get quick first opinions from what they see. It is very difficult to supersede that first impression. Think about offices you've been in where you had positive or negative impressions and what led you to that, and then set up your décor accordingly. Further, your office is your workspace – make sure it is comfortable, serviceable, and convenient for you. A trend in offices is to bring clients into antiseptic conference rooms that don't display any personality at all. Also, an advantage of meeting in a conference room is that you aren't forced to put away the work on your desk to keep it confidential.

Cars are important if they are noticed. A clunker or very expensive car would be noticed. You don't need to be into expensive or fancy cars, but you shouldn't drive something that might cause you to be embarrassed if a client sees you getting in or out of it. There are many cars to choose from and they don't seem to change their look every year. Get something a little above mid-range and you should be okay. Try to pick a model whose image would be just as good in a period of prosperity or a recession. Oh, and wash the outside and vacuum the inside regularly.

Another factor in offices and cars is the virtual office and social media. Many firms now operate without offices but through a network of connected cloud activities. I know a couple of very successful accountants – Jody Padar and Jason Blumer (you can find them easily through Google) – who are using this model to the nth degree. They blog, tweet, and give very enthusiastic web-based presentations. There are others, but they come quickly to mind.

More and more clients are connected, don't want to spend more time than absolutely necessary interacting with people who are not part of their core business and find that phone and webcast meetings are just as intimate as face-to-face. We are going through a new iteration of business that may or may not replace what we have become accustomed to, but is being adopted at an accelerated pace. In view of this, I suggest hopping aboard and getting comfortable with it. It saves time, reduces rent, and can be more effective in the right circumstances. A comment is that most of my discussions with Partners' Network callers are over the phone with quick email follow-up of materials when necessary – very little face to face but I seem to have satisfied callers, and I am sure this is so with you and your clients. Also most of us have attended webinars and were able to ask questions more easily than if we were at an in-person audience program. My firm now offers most of its in-house CPE programs online with no reduction of benefits and results.

Oh, many people run their office off an iPhone® or iPad®. And at some point this next new thing is already here – we really have to be ready to adapt and adopt.

One story if I may brag. Back in 1986 when desktop computers started to come down in price and our firm was doing more of its work that way, we started noticing that some of our staff were beginning to purchase PCs for their houses. I spoke with my partners about contributing to the cost and we decided that we would not and saw it as a commitment by them to be state of the art and to have the purchase as their participation in their training. One day a staff person told me he was going to get a PC and asked if we would help him out with part of the payment. When I told him no, he smirked and laughed a little. When I asked him what was so funny he replied, "At other firms this would be an enhancement in my status. Here I need to get one to keep up!" I felt as proud of my staff as I ever could at that moment. Today, at WS+B we provide every staff person with a laptop and iPhone®. But we also support BYOD (bring your own device) where staff can buy what they want to use and we will load it with our software, access codes, systems and security. What's next?

81. Charging Clients Late Fees

This question was originally sent to my partner Frank Boutillette.

Q:

You state on the bottom of the invoice that you charge 1. 5% for balances over 60 days. Do you actually implement that or is it just warning?

Do you do it on all clients or just some? Do clients pay that or complain? If they send in payment without that, do you write off the finance charge or leave it open? Also, is that mentioned in your engagement letter and when you started it did you send out some type of announcement? Does it work in getting clients to pay on time?

A:

We have been adding late charges on our bills for years. The wording is similar to this:

• Fees are payable as billed. There will be an additional charge of 1. 5% per month for past due balances.

We collect reasonable amounts of late fees. It is included in all engagement letters and is automatically added to all bills that are 60 days past due. If they send in payment without it, we usually write off the late charges. When clients complain about it, we try to get the payment, but will retreat either fully or partially if we get an immediate check with the assurance by the client that all future bills will be paid timely. If clients have very large past due balances (shame on us) and we work out a payment arrangement, usually where we charge their credit card on a regular basis, we tell them we will suspend the late charges and will cancel a portion or the previously added late charges when a certain agreed-upon amount is finally paid. In effect, it is a negotiating lever. If you never did it before, I suggest including it on the bottom of all your invoices for three months with the effective date before you start the automatic charging of the late charge. It definitely works in getting faster payment. But, I'll tell you what works better – calling the client three weeks after you sent the bill if it hasn't been paid yet. Don't let unpaid bills accumulate – it is bad business and sends the client a message that you are a bad businessperson. That is not a good image for a business advisor.

Five Clauses to Clarify and Protect

Following are some other clauses that can be considered for a proposal or engagement letter.

1. We also include the following in our engagement letters. (However, we do not include this in attestation assignments since it might be construed as a "contingent" fee.)

- We will also be entitled to an additional fee of $25,000 for any of our staff people you hire or engage to perform services for you.

2. The following language can be inserted in your engagement letters to limit your liability, although we do not do this. This clause limits your liability to fees paid. If you are concerned about this, check with your malpractice insurance carrier. I do not know the legality of this limitation, but it certainly cannot hurt to include it in your engagement letters.

- I will not be responsible to you or any third party, in damages or otherwise, for any loss, claim, damage or liability you may incur as a result of the services to be provided under this agreement, except to the extent that such loss, claim, damage or liability results from my willful misconduct or gross negligence. I will not be responsible in any amount in excess of the amounts paid under this agreement.

3. The following sentence limits the period the quoted fee is valid and sets a deadline for action.

- I sincerely appreciate this opportunity to be of service to you. If the above accurately reflects the terms and conditions of my engagement, please sign the enclosed letter and return it along with the retainer to me. The offer expires September XX, 20XX.

4. Here is yet another clause that could be included in engagement letters for fixed-fee engagements.

- While the fixed price entitles your company to unlimited consultation with us, if your question or issue requires additional research and analysis beyond the consultation, that work will be subject to additional fees, which will be determined by both of us before the service is to be performed.

5. Clause for value or additional billing after the services have been performed

- We base our fees on time required at our regular rates for the type of se5. vices and personnel assigned plus out-of-pocket costs. We also consider the difficulty and size of the assignment, the degree of skill required, the experience and ability of the personnel assigned, time limitations imposed on us by others, the nature of the project, the level of cooperation by the client's staff, and the value of the services to the client.

82. Project Management

Q:

I assigned four projects to a manager who reassigned them to a Staff 2 person and I gave a date when they were needed that was three weeks away.

When I asked about the progress after two weeks, I was told that nothing was near completion. Now there is a super rush with much stress.

How could this situation have been avoided?

A:

First off – you are to blame. You did not work with the manager to see how she would assign the work and to whom. You did not need to micromanage, but could have made some big-picture assessments of the reality of getting the jobs done on time. Also you should have inquired about the progress after a few days up to a week – two weeks is too long to go without an update.

Now, let's talk about the manager. This person clearly doesn't know how to manage multiple priorities. It is a fault of you and your partners that this person was put in a manager position without the basic management skills.

Was she taught how to manage, or did she acquire her skills by osmosis from you, which, based on what I wrote in the previous paragraph, is somewhat deficient? I don't want to sound hard, but when you called your first comments were to blame the Staff 2, who I think is least to blame. When things go wrong, the problem's genesis is usually at the top, not the bottom.

The Staff 2 did not know how to handle the multiple projects. There was no instruction on his proposed time management and scheduling. It seems there was instruction to make sure he had the ability to handle the work from a skill standpoint, but that is not the problem here. Also, the jobs were assigned at different times without asking him about his workload.

The manager assigning the work should have been aware of the workload since she assigned to him all four jobs, but she did not connect the dots. She got the projects off her desk, gave them to someone she knew could do the work and then walked away. It turns out the Staff 2 apportioned his time so he worked on each of the four jobs equal amounts of time each day. This was his way of dealing with the multiple assignments – equal time for all. This sort of guaranteed that nothing would be completed on time.

He also had too many touches, making the time on each project longer than if he worked straight through one until completion and then on to the next job. In this manner, perhaps two jobs would have been completed with a third one partway done.

When the partner finally looked at the situation, he could have given the unstarted job to someone else, allowing the Staff 2 to complete the third project he already started. In this manner, at least three jobs would have been completed and probably the fourth job.

Project management – it works, but needs effort, focus, oversight and training – not osmosis.

83. ■ Writing a book

Q:

I want to write a book. How do I go about it?

A:

You go about it in an organized step-by-step basis. Following is a brief checklist of how to get started.

How to Write a Book in Eight Steps

1. Decide on topic

2. Determine a working title

3. Prepare an outline of the topics you will cover – show each topic as a chapter

4. Write up a "business plan" with the following topics answered

   a. Book summary

   b. Purpose of writing the book, i. e. ego, establish yourself as an expert, share experiences or knowledge, gain fame or customers, business promotion, make money

c. Why there is a need for your book

d. Audience for book

e. Theme of book

f. What makes the book different

g. Why you are qualified to write the book

h. Estimated size of book – number of pages or words

i. Similar books in the market and what makes your book different and better

j. People who can endorse the book

5. Write an introduction and two sample chapters

6. A strategy to locate an agent or editor is to identify similar books or books targeted to your audience, and look at the acknowledgements and contact those agents and editors. Assume you will only have one shot at them, so prepare a complete proposal before contacting them

7. Decide whether you will self-publish the book if you cannot get a conventional publisher

8. Think about appropriate cover art

There is more after that, such as preparing the proposal to obtain an agent or publisher, a possible marketing plan, research that might be needed, and copyright clearances for material you want to include in your book.

As you write, do not concern yourself with the grammar, proofing or editing. You can hire people to do this or the publisher will arrange for this. But your ideas and thoughts must be clear.

If you want to self-publish the book, determine the maximum cost you will want to pay. You can get an idea by going to createspace. com. That site also has author guides you can download and review.

Almost no book makes money, and most of the ones that do have focused marketing supporting the book. If you self-publish and do not arrange for the marketing, it is unlikely the book will recover its costs. You also need to become an "expert" in social media that can drive sales of your book.

84. Mitigating Risk in New Services

Q:

I want to get more involved in a broader range of services. How do you think I should get started?

A:

I've written a number of Q&As on this. However, new things keep popping up, so I am responding to this question here, but won't be covering things I wrote already about.

This person was interested in getting involved in mergers and acquisitions, particularly because he heard that fees can be much higher than hourly rates and based on value created, or "points. " He is right about that. The bigger the transaction you are involved in and add to, the greater the potential for higher fees. However, there is a downside and that is the exposure to liability.

One of my partners sent an email as part of our conflict-check process, saying:

> *We have been referred to serve as for a forensic accountant to assist in a lawsuit claiming fraud, breach of contract and misrepresentation from the purchase of a business. We would be representing the purchaser who is suing the seller. Their financial advisors have also been named in the suit.*

You cannot prevent being sued, especially when one side thinks they got a bad deal. What you can do is mitigate your exposure or even prevent yourself from losing, such as...

19 Tips on How Not to Lose a Lawsuit

1. Take courses and attend lectures and presentations by experts in the technical area AND industry you work in. For example, if you value a construction contractor and haven't taken any courses in the previous ten years on industry trends you can be exposed and have little defense about your expertise

2. Subscribe to and read professional and trade journals

3. Have clients in the industry or profession, and meet regularly with them to discuss industry issues

4. Present speeches and CPE programs, and write articles, on your area of expertise

5. Join and participate in professional committees on the topics

6. Join and participate in client trade organizations

7. Get to know the players in the industry or profession – become a go-to person. A great way to keep up to date is to have people call you with questions. It tells you what are current issues and concerns and forces you to think about them so you can provide a clear response. If you don't know the answer, it gives you an opportunity to find out something maybe you should know about. You can reach out to your go-to person for their responses. That is why I want calls from colleagues. You all keep me on my toes!

8. If you use staff to assist you, depending upon their level, the above could also apply to them

9. You need engagement letters clearly defining what you will be doing, your responsibility and the client's responsibility

10. If you do not receive requested documentation and proceed by working around it or provide alternative procedures, you should amend the engagement letter, or issue a new one, or present a change order to client. Do not be trapped in by scope creep. When you extend your services, you create an implied impression that you are stepping up to responsibility for the success of the work you do

11. If you work with other professionals, make sure the arrangement and scope is clear

12. When you do your work, you should clearly document what you did with backup and the reasons that drew you to your conclusions

13. You must properly supervise those assisting you

14. You must meet all time commitments and requirements – do not dilly dally. If never hurts (almost never) to get things done quickly. You should never be the person others are waiting on

15. Have any deliverables proof read

16. Make sure all facts are correct

17. When you give an opinion, make sure it is presented as an opinion and that you were engaged to offer that opinion

18. If you are engaged as an expert to present an opinion, make sure you don't become an advocate for one side of the transaction

19. If something looks like a high risk situation, with litigious clients, and you are not thoroughly confident in the issues, walk away!

Following all of these points may not stop you from losing the suit, but they provide a strong defense of your competence or ability.

85. Being Judged Based On The Clients You Have

Q:

We all know that we are being judged by who our clients are by everyone we meet, even if it is subconscious. How does this matter? And does it affect growth?

A:

I think it matters and proof of it is how many CPAs and other professionals brag about or name-drop who some of their clients are. I have found that almost every accountant has at least one client that they can name drop. Prestige comes with who uses you. If a famous, rich or known successful person uses you, you must be great.

It also works in reverse. If you have a lot of low-end (or low life) clients and it becomes known, you then get judged by them. I once moved in to share an office with a CPA I thought very highly of. Once in his office and I saw the type of clients that came in and out of his office, I lost respect for him and quickly found a reason to extricate myself from that arrangement.

Working on big or intricate transactions or for mega rich clients also creates feelings of confidence as does with well known professionals in other fields. Mentioning that you have a client that had a building named after him or who got an honorary degree from a prestigious university is impressive as is mentioning someone famous that got their start with help from you.

It has become commonplace for prospective clients to ask for references and industry specific clients. Our firm provides actual client names in many of our proposals. Obviously we are not listing marginal organizations.

Of course, never reveal anything specific about a client or associate a client with a particular transaction that you may have talked about.

People like to work with and associate with successful people. You are judged by the company you keep.

86. Keeping Track of Other Professionals

Q:

How can I keep track of the various professionals my clients use as a method of cross referrals?

A:

I have a pretty simple method that works. I keep folders in a file drawer in my desk labeled for each type of professional I want to keep track of –

- lawyers,
- insurance brokers and agents,
- real estate brokers,
- bankers,
- investment bankers,
- stock brokers,
- financial planners and money managers,
- other CPAs, and
- reporters and editors.

Whenever I come across someone I put their contact info in the appropriate folder. This includes letterhead, brochures and business cards – something that will remind me of how I met them and common relationship if any.

I also put them on my firm's mailing list categorized by profession. Some might think it's overkill, but the folder has the information about how we met or interacted. The mailing list is good to segregate groups for promotional purposes, mailings and calls. Sometimes many years pass before there is a second contact and having a descriptive piece of paper in front of me helps jogged the memory.

I also try to keep track of birthdays, hobbies and special interests. I try to do this for everyone I know. When the opportunity presents itself I call or email a birthday wish and send a hobby or related item I come across. Those who know me know I am very promotion-minded – and these contacts work. I have a big bag of tricks – but they are useless without the list.

By the way, instead of folders you can keep files on your computer. I tried this but I still like the paper method better.

87. ■ Out of Control

Q:

Sometimes I feel I am out of control. Any suggestions?

A:

I think everyone in business at times feels out of control. Simple things mount up and cause some pressure.

It works to make a habit of keeping things in order, not letting things pile up and following my rules:

Do It Now! Touch it Once! Concentrate on your Most Important Thing!

Here is a short list of some things that can put you or keep you in control:

- Keep desk clean

- Open postal mail and take care of, assign, file or toss. Neat piles become tomorrow's mess

- Do the same with emails – open, take care of, assign, file or delete

- Return (or have someone return) all phone calls – phone calls can also be returned with e-mails and you don't have to ask how their weekend or vacation was

- Schedule work realistically and keep promises or let people know early on that a commitment cannot be met and reschedule it

• Establish checklists and written procedures and make sure they are followed

• Know what your staff is doing and that they are doing the right thing at the right time the right way

• Your staff needs to report to you on schedule and meet deadlines and use checklist and follow procedures

• Partners need to get back to staff with open items, answers to questions, and their schedules need to be respected

• Think and be orderly

88. ■ Moonlighting Staff

Q:

I suspect a key staff person is moonlighting and is building up a sizable tax season practice for himself. Should I confront him, or let it ride?

A:

I moonlighted, as I am sure many people in their own practice did. When I had my practice, I liked the fact that staff moonlighted and I encouraged it. They learned from the mistakes they made on their own returns, and I got the benefit of that.

The moonlighters were more diligent, on the ball, kept up to date better, were more process oriented, organized their time better, developed self-checking methods that upgraded the work they did for me, and were more "touchy-feely" with clients reducing the time I needed to spend with some of my clients.

The downside is that they had an eye on starting their own practice, and could not spend as much time as I might have wanted them to working overtime for me, although they all worked the required overtime hours.

I spoke to them and told them that it was alright for them to moonlight, and that if they had questions or problems, they should ask me for help. If they only did a few returns, I also told them they could use our software as long as they removed our name as preparer.

Not one to let something go, I explained what I saw as the benefits to them and to us, but that from a money standpoint, they probably would make as much working the extra hours for us rather than moonlighting. We paid straight time for hours over 40 worked in a week. I also pointed out their additional costs – computer software, malpractice insurance, separate PTIN, FedEx charges and general administrative costs.

89. Referral from a Bad Accountant

Q:

I was referred a client by another CPA, a friend who felt he had a conflict representing that client.

I was appreciative and glad to get the client.

However, once I started work, the quality of what he gave me that I had to pick up on was terrible. I tried covering for him, but it caused me to spend much more time than I thought I would and for which I wasn't getting paid for.

How do I handle continuing work on this client and also keep my friendship?

A:

Been there, done that. And it sucks.

On some level you have a responsibility to not make the referring CPA look bad. On another level, you also have a responsibility to get paid for your work. You can do nothing and go with the flow of the situation; drop the client; or ask for a greater fee. Enlisting the CPA to do some back up corrective work might not be a good idea. What you decide has to be based on what you feel is good business for you in the long range.

You have to make the decision. It's tough! One tip: each situation is different and even though this did not work out, it doesn't mean that the next ones won't be successful. Also, this is really no different than when you get a new client and their accounting is all messed up.

Regardless of the "low" fee and your "loss," you will be receiving cash fees that you would not have had. Think about that!

One tip is to protect the referral source!

90. 88% Effective Staff

Q:

I have some staff people that do adequate work, but not great or complete jobs.

It seems I always need to complete their work. I just can't get completed work. I also don't want to let them go. What I have works, but I don't seem to be growing. Any suggestions?

A:

Everyone has some staff that does not get the job completely done. And to make things more difficult, they are usually longer term employees who are very nice people who fit in well with your organization.

When you have staff, you delegate work, authority and representation. The successful people do it well, with proper management, empowerment and opportunity while maintaining the right culture.

Compromises need to be accepted. However, too many compromises thwart growth for you and your staff.

It is a shared endeavor and involves shared responsibilities. Yours are to provide reasonable pay and work conditions, management, opportunity and empowerment. Theirs is to work diligently, assume responsibility and to grow by taking over more of your work, learning new things and acquiring additional skills.

If you don't do your part neither you or your staff will grow. Likewise if they don't do their part.

Now let's get to the specific problem you asked me about. The staff person you asked me about hasn't grown because they did not step up to take full responsibility to complete their jobs. This is a long standing issue, so it would seem to me they had plenty of time to acquire the skills or realize they need to pay full attention to what is expected of them. I consider the staff person culpable. If they are let go, receive stunted raises, or become stagnated (without a clue) then that is their fault and deserve the consequences. On the other hand, you let a situation fester and not develop beyond the inadequate place it is now at. You're the boss – you are responsible, and you let yourself down as well as the staff person.

These comments describe the situation and place blame but do not provide a means to fix it. One way to start is to examine the situation based on what I just said and then work with the staff person to see that they grow into the completion phase. It wouldn't be easy and you might feel you already did it but there was no response. I would try again and at the same time reassess your abilities along with personal and firm goals. Perhaps you should also think about replacing them – add a person and see if they develop into the level you need – before you let the stagnant person go.

Growth can only come if you leverage your abilities through effective staff.

91. Partner Marketing or Selling

Q:

One of my partners is technically brilliant, does the work of 2½ people and always meets deadlines. My only complaint is that she never tries to get any new business. How can I get her to do some marketing?

A:

Partners need to market. They are business owners and cannot shirk performing some minimal marketing. It is obvious you are happy with her, that she is great to have around and can be relied on, but marketing is part of the game.

Many technically proficient partners (and other staff too) need to recognize that every interaction they have with a client or prospect is "marketing" and they should be prepped on how to handle it to result in additional business.

Prospecting and meeting potential clients takes effort and skill and opportunities should be recognized and taken advantage of. This also requires going out of your way. "Selling" additional services to existing clients is different. They know the firm and you and your capabilities, trust you, can reach you, and meet and speak to you on some sort of regular basis so have a comfort level with you.

Selling, like everything else you do, needs preparation. When you are going to meet with a client, develop a plan to discuss additional services they need that you could perform. Show them what they need, why, the value to them, the timing and cost, and possibly explain why it was never suggested previously. That is selling! Another selling effort is to ask for referrals. – not too hard, just ask if they know anyone that might benefit from meeting with you, and then sit quiet until they give you a name. That is also selling!

Partners should be accountable for fee increases and additional services for the clients they work on and referrals from them. The lack of any of these could indicate a level of dissatisfaction with your firm, and while the dissatisfaction is not serious enough for the client to leave, it is such that you are stuck at a level that isn't helping your firm to grow. You need to address the dissatisfaction, but that is for a different Q&A.

By the way, if you recommended an additional service, why wasn't it recommended earlier? Maybe that's why your client might be dissatisfied. And maybe the client might just welcome having that service? And even if they don't engage you for it, it extends your image beyond what you just do for them.

92. Value of an Outside Accountant

Q:

I have a client for which we prepare an annual Review Report. We also look at their quarterly QuickBooks® numbers before the client sends them to their bank. We almost always suggested some journal entries and we also discuss what we find with the client.

Another CPA does the tax returns for the business and owner. The client just paid off his bank loan and now questions whether he should still have us continue with the same services. What do I say to him?

A:

You lost it! You should know the value you add to his business and should be constantly letting client know how lucky they are having you as their accountant and advisor.

But to answer your question, here is what you should say, because it reflects the value of what you are doing…

"Our services provide an independent look that gives us an opportunity to catch anything that might be out of the ordinary; that makes your bookkeeper or accounting department aware there is oversight; and we do make changes or suggestions almost every time we look at your records. While we were a 'necessary evil' because of the bank, we provided a value to you that gave you comfort that your records were in order.

"In case you are not aware of exactly what we do, we review the reconciliations of your bank accounts, perform a monthly trend analysis each quarter. We don't just look at the quarterly numbers – we look at the monthly numbers each three months and we also look at the full year to date monthly P&Ls and Balance Sheets, and also compare them to the previous year.

"We don't just look at the P&L, but look for unusual changes in the balance sheet items which could indicate problems such as slowing accounts receivable or growing inventory which do not show up on the P&L reports.

"We also do some tax planning and make sure that your estimated taxes will be adequate and if not, we contact your tax accountant with the information.

"The bank wanted us to perform these services not only to give them a better reliance on the numbers you submit, but to assure you have access to a 'consultant' should that need arise.

"The fact that you haven't had problems is in some measure to your good management and our oversight. There is a great value to what we do, and it should be maintained. "

Before you can respond to the client you have to be clear of the many things you do and benefits to the client. You can also look at the above response and make up a checklist of things to do if you aren't already doing these services.

Actually, you can only say something of value if you provide value, and then you won't be asked about the value you provide – it will be ubiquitous.

Sometimes I get carried away with a project. And following is evidence of that. The way things work are sometimes very coincidental. Besides the person calling me with this question, I spoke to three accountants who wanted suggestions of additional services they could offer to business clients, as an extra – something that would not take too much time and would have high impact.

Here's where I got carried away. I made up a checklist of some of these things. You can pick two or three things each time you perform any other services for that client.

Use the checklist as a guide or follow it – but there are enough things here to get you started pretty quickly.

78 Potential Value-Add Services

Purpose of this checklist

This checklist is a guide to jog additional thought about the client's business. You can choose to work on a few items each time you perform services for the client as a value added benefit to the client, or use checklist as a guide for a separate engagement. Either way, your emphasis should be to provide information to the client about their business that they do not already consider, focus in on or know

General

1. Does client receive timely financial statements?

2. Does the client really understand the financial statement?

3. How up to date is the bookkeeping and accounting?

4. Review client's financial controls and cash flow

5. What is the quality of the internal controls on the client's business?

6. If the client uses Key Performance Indicators, review a listing of most recent amounts with client

7. If more than one owner, get a copy of the buy-sell agreement. If no agreement, ask why

Risk management

8. Review client's insurance policies to determine if coverage is adequate

9. Compare inventory insurance limit with actual inventory amount and compare to inventory at highest level during the year (particularly if business is seasonal)

10. Determine if there is coverage for "new" items such as Internet theft, electronic embezzlement, copyright and patent infringement and accusations of sex and other types of workplace harassment or discrimination

11. Review with client security of physical assets

12. Does company have secure firewalls for computer spam?

13. Is there secure offsite backup of servers and digital data? How often is data backed up and is it automatic and how often is it tested to be working properly?

14. Is there a continuation plan if premises are destroyed, say by a fire?

15. Are all software licenses in order and updated?

16. Is the primary owner/manager covered for life and disability insurance with the business the beneficiary?

17. Given the nature of the business, has client considered potential for risks, i. e. things that could occur that will impact the functioning of the business, and devised plans to overcome them?

Cash flow

18. Do a working capital analysis

19. Do a quick ratio analysis and other ratio analyses

20. Review operational ratios and relate to cash flow and stagnant cash generating items

21. Review debt to equity ratio and discuss adequacy with client

22. Get copies of budget and long range projection, if any

23. Get capital expenditures budget for next few years

24. Determine how client keeps track of cash receipts, disbursements and balances

25. Review large accounts receivable customer balances

Sales

26. Review the client's five or ten largest customers and their buying and payments patterns

27. Perform an 80/20 review of the client's customers

28. A review of sales returns, allowances, markdowns, and debits to determine if there is a pattern from any customer, or any sales person's customers

29. Determine the amount of time from shipment that a sale is returned

30. Discuss with client and get a sense of their pricing policies, strategies, methods and formulas

31. Determine how often and when client increases their prices and if not done, initiate a discussion with the client on why, when and how to raise prices

32. Identify the different types or groups of customers

33. How does the client distinguish between types or groups of customers?

34. Estimate the average invoice size this year compared to prior years

35. Try to track some of the largest selling items over the last five years

Production

36. How does the client dispose of stale inventory?

37. What is the order backlog situation?

38. Identify production bottlenecks

39. When was the last time the client took a walk through the factory, shipping area, and other essential areas, or how often is it done?

40. Does client use video cameras in production and inventory areas?

41. Is there a small number of essential suppliers, or a wide range? Review a list of five largest vendors.

42. How important to the business are the top five suppliers?

43. Has the client recently compared the prices a client pays for raw materials with competitive suppliers' prices?

44. Review prices paid for consistency with the supplier? How often do the prices change?

45. Review some production reports

46. What does the client measure?

47. Identify salient product lines – e. g. US vs. Metric sizes? How do these compare. What is the growth of metric? Is US losing ground more rapidly than sales dollars indicate? How much metric sizes do they actually deliver in U. S.

48. Is inventory primarily current items. Measure inventory turnover by product line

49. How much inventory is very slow moving items

50. Did you indicate possible cost of retaining old inventory

Payroll

51. How stable is the labor force. Is there much turnover?

52. Get a listing of 5 highest paid employees and discuss with client

53. What type of people is the client hiring now compared to five years ago

54. If there is a labor union how are relations with the union?

55. If the client is not unionized, what is the client doing to keep it that way?

56. How has production per employee changed over the last five years?

57. What is the age range for key employees – is there effective back up for older people, and is there a plan to transfer knowledge to younger staff?

Value of Business

58. Does Company have a recent valuation?

59. What is client's estimate of the value?

60. Is that greater or lower than five years ago?

61. What's client's estimate for five years from now?

62. How would you value the business?

63. Explain to client why it is important to have a current valuation – insurance, financing, exit planning, measure growth in value, determine trend and viability of business, identify value drivers, isolate intangible value, look at market position and brand value

64. Try to identify with client circumstances that caused or can cause value to change

65. Examples to consider – types of customers, i. e. OEMs, distributors, retail or web based; order size, JIT orders, customer complaints or service issues

66. Factor in value of business to owners' individual financial plans

67. Discuss with client how a valuation creates a big picture perspective and moves thinking away from daily activities

Client's future

68. What are the long-term prospects for the client's industry?

69. How is the client preparing for the future?

70. Is the client making investments in equipment and technology?

71. Discuss with the client what their goals are, why they are in business

72. Discuss the client's transition plans and/or exit strategy with them. Note: a client without an effective exit strategy may not be organized as well as it should be.

73. Discuss with the client what would happen to the business if they or their partner got sick, or died?

74. Has client had a business retreat?

75. Has client developed forward thinking strategies?

76. Find out how well the client is adapting to change

77. Are the client's management techniques still applicable?

78. Determine if the client's emphasis is for them to lead or to manage. "Lead" indicates the client has a strategy and that the client wants the right things done. "Manage" indicates they want things done the way things are supposed to be done but doesn't necessarily mean the right things are being done. Either way, the client should be able to explain what's important is them and how they are involved in the daily functioning of the business.

93. ■ Keeping Current

Q:

I find it hard to keep current, and am inundated with snail mail and emails. How do you do it?

A:

I have a lot of suggestions, but the truth of the matter is I also get overwhelmed with the material I receive.

I maintain every AICPA specialty and need to take CPE in each area. Additionally I attend about three national CPE conferences a year covering about 60 CPE credits, give a dozen speeches a year, write 100 blogs and 60 Q&As a year, yadda yadda yadda…

I try to focus my time to learn what is new – not to learn the topic, but to know about it. I've gotten into the habit of looking most everything up and because of this *I don't have to know anything but have to know about everything.*

I am stingy with my "learning" time, choosing to spend it where I get the biggest return on my investment.

Let me give you three examples.

Example 1:

I belong to the National Association of Tax Professionals. They have a monthly journal that has a few short articles that are really good and thorough on specific tax topics. I can go through an issue in a couple of minutes, resisting the urge to read everything, but glancing so I know what topics are covered. I get a gist of the new tax issues and keep them in a file folder in a desk drawer. When I need to know more about a tax topic I go through this file easily retrieving the issue with the article that will lay out what I need to know. For heavier research, I use this as a starting point – it is focused and direct and cuts a lot of time off of my work.

I also have a bi-weekly subscription to *PPC Practitioners Tax Action Bulletins* and use it the same way. I get the mail subscription and use these bulletins the same way. These are much more voluminous and contain more information and a ton of checklists. (I really like checklists.) Because it is much more expensive than the NATP membership, I recommend the NATP first, and if you are really involved in tax research, I suggest looking into the PPC Tax Alerts.

Example 2:

I subscribe to *The Accounting Daily* blog and Tweet aggregator. It is free and I get a daily email around 11:00 am. This contains headlines and very brief summaries of anywhere from 80 to 150 blogs, tweets and articles.

Looking quickly I spot items I am interested in, click and read and where necessary, copy and paste in a Word file I set up to retain such articles for later retrieval. When I need to retrieve something I saved, I do a word search and it gets me the article with the subject I am interested in.

Looking at *The Accounting Daily* eliminates my having to go through numerous emails I get each day from a myriad of sources that are picked up here. Also, because I subscribe to *The Accounting Daily*, I do not have to receive many other emails that contain ads and where my email address might be shared with related sources cutting down on some emails I receive. A link to them is: cpaclick. com/kopptweets.

CPA Trendlines also aggregates the day's news from the leading tax, accounting and finance media authorities in a twice-a-day email, at cpaclick. com/cpa-daily

Example 3:

I regularly clip articles from journals, newsletters and other publications on topics I am interested in. I file them (informally) in some sort of order that allows me to retrieve them, by category, when I need them. These clippings are from an earlier generation than the Word file described in Example 2.

The trick is not to allow your mail to accumulate. Maintaining a "pile" is worse than worthless since it consumes space and time, and is a distraction.

94. Preparing a Client Newsletter

Q:

I am contemplating issuing a monthly newsletter that I can forward to my contacts and clients.

The objective is to establish and promote my expertise in a format that can be easily distributed. Each newsletter would consist of a brief commentary on a topic of my choosing (an economic, financial, or business management issue - I will avoid politics whenever possible) and a summary of a tax topic that is relevant to business owners and/or wealthy individuals. As I know you maintain a successful and quite useful blog, and thanks for the many checklists, I am seeking general advice, do's/do not's, that you might have to offer.

A:

Newsletters are a method of making clients aware of areas of firm expertise, firm news, specialized information appealing to a segment of clients, and tax and accounting changes. Newsletters can also highlight interesting client businesses and special interests of the partners and staff.

Our newsletters also had contests and other devises designed to create a sense of community, credibility and trust for the firm, and to provide the client something with our name on it that hopefully would sit on their desk for a week or two. Since the newsletter was mailed, we were able to control, and know, who received it. We weren't able to control whether it was opened and then read, but we included things that elicited responses and were happy with those response rates. For example, when we offered something of interest for free, we got a large number of replies, and our financial indicator contests always had over 130 participants with many more readers commenting on it when we met with them. Newsletters also offer a permanent record of the firm.

I always like sending things to clients that have a shelf life, i. e. something that would sit on their desk for a while. Newsletters are one of those things. A prior issue is also something you can send to a client or prospect quickly with information about a subject area that interest has been expressed in.

Newsletters can be postal mailed or emailed. WS+B does both. I keep an inventory of extra copies that I can mail to people and often email specific articles. Our web site withum. com has prior issues of the Journals easily available.

One article I email a lot is by Sara Palovick on *New Baby Tax Benefits* to people that just had a baby or new grandchild. Newsletters can also promote firm events such as seminars and webinars, publications you provide articles to, books you contributed to or wrote, awards staff and partners received, and charitable boards staff and partners serve on.

We also have specialized newsletters for the many niches we have and promote. These are primarily emailed with hard copies available to give to people. We use single subject alerts that are prepared and emailed quickly. Email has greatly reduced the delivery time and cost, but doesn't substitute, in my opinion, for the touchy-feely relationship a properly prepared newsletter provides. I believe that a high percentage of people receiving emailed newsletters do not open them while I think the reverse is true of postal mailed newsletters.

Note that the *Partners' Network Newsletter* is mailed and emailed. We find we get much greater feedback from the postal mailed issue justifying the added costs.

Many organizations prepare newsletters that CPAs can purchase with their firm names printed on it, and some even will customize portions, so you don't have to be a great writer to get one done.

I like newsletters and think they work for the right purposes. I also think that blogs have partially replaced newsletters for technical information. In 2004 I presented a day long practice management conference for the NJSCPAs and spent quite a bit of time discussing the advantages of publishing a firm newsletter.

Things change. Today I would spend a little less time on newsletters and added time on the various types and uses of social media.

Newsletters are not an end but part of a comprehensive marketing program. That needs to be kept in mind when considering using them.

95. Reasons for CPA Firm Mergers

Q:

There seems to be many CPA practice mergers but I have had a few conversations with other firms and don't understand how they can all become successful.

I am a small firm – two partners and nine employees and, except for some cost savings, I don't see how there can be suitable growth so I could make enough more money to make it worthwhile giving up the control and great partner relationship I have now. What are your thoughts?

A:

I've written many Q&As on this issue and this area generates a large number of calls. Here are some more thoughts that haven't already appeared in a Q&A.

Mergers seem to be a major growth strategy for larger CPA firms. It is practically in their DNA.

Large practices need to grow to provide opportunities for staff, greater compensation for partners, acquire rather than grow specialists, keep up with client growth and changing need for additional services, expansion of partnership admissions of younger partners to have a larger pool of people able to make the retirement or buyout payments to the older partners, consolidation of resources, greater capital to invest in infrastructure and marketing, expand geographic area of practice, and a larger pool of partners with expertise to manage and run the firm when the managing partners retire. Sometimes the merger is to wake up a tired group of staff and partners.

Power within many CPA firms is through control of clients and through rainmaking. Mistakenly, many firms choose the most powerful partners to run the practice rather than someone more qualified and disposed for the task. Also, you are removing someone from putting all their efforts into what they do best for the firm to do something that more likely can be done better by someone else? This situation leads many firms to a tailspin – not so vigorous – by a curtailing of growth or a decline in growth. And this leads logically to a merger where they can go back to what they do best and the management is handled by someone already proven in that discipline. Also, just because someone is a top rainmaker doesn't mean they are a good leader.

Many larger firms try to "be all things to all clients" with a full range of services and in house experts. This can't always be grown and merging with firms with that expertise accelerates the process.

Many firms turn down work or refer it elsewhere. Measuring that potential volume can provide a strong basis for bringing in someone to do that work internally.

Why We Merged

I can cite three examples that caused me to want to merge, before we merged with WS+B.

The first is when we were turning down a large amount of peer reviews because we did not have Yellow Book experience. At first we accepted those reviews and had another firm do the Yellow Book reviews for us. It got to the point where we were being charged almost as much for that review as we were charging for the entire peer review. Not good business so we had to turn down those peer reviews. We were looking to either merge with a smaller firm that did Yellow Book audits, or hire someone with that experience – neither happened.

A second was when we took on a public company audit because of an entwined client relationship and we did not want them working with another CPA firm. We tried to merge with a small firm performing a reasonable number of these audits, but could not find a firm with the quality of review procedures we felt was necessary.

The third was to bring in a smaller practitioner with certain strong qualities that we were weak in. While we were very compatible and are still in close touch with him, a merger did not seem to be able to be consummated.

Other reasons we considered were because a couple of clients were growing rapidly with expanding credit lines and we felt a merger with a larger CPA firm would help retain those clients.

We bought a number of practices, and referred to the transaction as a merger, but in reality, we acquired the client base and the selling owners went bye-bye. I think many smaller CPA firm mergers are really sales.

96. ■ Succession Planning for CPAs

Q:

I am 57 and have become very concerned about retiring and what I could get for my practice, how long I would have to stay and how the whole process works.

Is there anything you can give me that sort of ties in everything?

A:

For CPAs in practice, succession planning takes on a meaning other than what it might seem. Many of the CPAs I know find it difficult to imagine themselves retiring, and therefore do little in the way of planning.

For those who think they will work until they drop, stop reading now and go to a Sudoku puzzle, because that will probably provide you with more gratification in the long run.

CPAs usually assume that either younger partners or long-time employees will "buy them out," or that they will sell or merge their practice when they are ready to retire.

Most CPA firm buyout arrangements are substantially unfunded. There is no buildup of funds to make the payments. The payments are made out of the future earnings of the practice.

In a large measure, the payments are contingent on the ability and desire of the remaining partners to make the payments. To the extent that they are funded, it is usually with the retiring partner's own funds during the period they are active with the practice.

In many instances there is an expectation gap between the retiring and the acquiring partners. In some situations, the buyers are paying for what they built, while in others they are taking over something where they have never been treated as anything other than "low-level" employees.

Either way, the person leaving assumes one thing and the successors assume something else.

A good plan has to balance this. If not, then problems will arise for both sides.

An agreement has to be drafted so that payments can easily be made and expected; the client base remains secure and firm; and the retired partner can remain retired while the successors become "unbossed."

Determining an Exit Strategy

There is an inherent conflict between wanting the best deal when you exit and wanting the best arrangement during the time you are working. Most people generally cannot have both.

Accepting that, practitioners then have to decide whether to set up their business in the manner that best fits their personal wishes and work styles and maximizes their present income, or that potentially maximizes the back-end value.

The trade-off is that one might not get as much for the practice in the back end as one could, or would, like to get. Most people are not aware that they are making a choice or that a choice been made for them by default.

To give you an example, if you were to build the practice in a way that maximizes your exit, it would most likely cost you more currently, and inhibit the way you might want to work.

With a current strategy, the focus is on you, the staff and the overhead structure that you are comfortable with. Your choice of staff would suit your work style, and your desire to optimize current income.

If you let an exit strategy drive the decisions, you might look to acquire staff suitable to buying you out. You might also need a more experienced staff and perhaps people qualified to buy you out sometime, or at a fixed time, in the future.

Instead of having good people in the right position, with the criteria being how well they perform, you would need to evaluate people on how well they can bring in business and handle clients, carry on in your absence or how able they might be in the future to make exit payments to you.

Also, in that type of environment, every new hire would have to be viewed as being something other or more than you would presently need.

Let's put a price on that. If the extra annual costs for the next 15 years would be $50,000, $250,000 or another value, depending upon the size of the practice, in order to enable you to be properly bought out it would cost you $750,000 or more. Is that money you could recoup?

Also, there is no guarantee that this would work out. There is a big assumption here that the right people are available and just waiting to buy you out, and will be able to buy you out when you decide to retire.

And what happens if you have to retire prematurely? Or, what if the people you have chosen die prematurely?

Firm Value

The value of a practice is illusory and only meaningful if it is sold and you receive the payments you are supposed to.

We are in a service business with no tangible product. Our reputation is our major asset. One large lawsuit can put us out of business, as could a series of large-client losses, a serious illness such as a stroke or heart disease, a tragic car accident or a spouse's debilitating illness.

And there is no denying that we get old. We may not feel old, and may have more energy than those half our age, but the perception of younger clients is that we are not for them. The longer you live, the longer your practice's value will dwindle.

The asset value of the practice looks good on a personal financial statement, but only the cash flow from the sale will have any meaning to you, and even those amounts have shrunk over the last few years from 1 1/2 to 2 X gross to 1 (or less) X gross with some manner of client-retention guarantees.

A loss of clients during the guarantee period would diminish the future payments for the practice. In most situations, the loss is beyond the control of the seller.

Merging the practice as a prelude to your retirement should provide a greater valuation because the retention would be greater the longer the eventual retiree stays on, though that involves working for a boss during the transition period.

The type of practice also plays a key part in the valuation. An individual tax or a small business client practice would be valued differently from a financial statement audit practice or a practice specializing in not-for-profit clients.

The Bottom Line

The bottom line is that we love being accountants, we love the work we do, and for many it is a real passion. And many have no plans for retirement.

The best planning you can do now for your retirement or succession is to try to organize your practice so that your physical presence is not needed for the work to get done.

Though you should maintain a physical presence necessary with clients, this can be phased out in favor of retirement as long as your partners and staff are on top of, and in control of, the work.

Most of us have no serious concerns about retirement and feel that when that day comes we will know it and deal with it then. The most important thing to remember is that this is a process and it does involve some early planning to increase the buyout you will receive.

– The preceding was first published as an article by me by the NYSSCPA *Trusted* Professional *and is adapted here with permission*

97. ■Managing Partner by Default

Q:

I am the managing partner of my accounting firm by default. No one else wanted to do it.

I am trying to manage things but I have a full schedule, am shorthanded on staff, and continue to do a reasonable amount of marketing. I am overwhelmed. How do others do it?

A:

I purposely left off the size of the firm because my response applies to every size firm – those with two partners on up to large firms with upwards of fifty partners. No matter the size of your practice, it is a business and needs someone dedicated to running it. Smaller firms need less time, possibly less skills and perhaps one of the partners can fill in this role. Larger firms need a person that spends substantially all of their time running the business, but not necessarily a partner.

Let's start with small firms. Running the business means making sure clients are serviced properly, timely, profitably and in accordance with the arrangements made with the client, bills go out on time; collections are prompt; staff are scheduled appropriately and timely based on their level and skills; staff are trained properly so they can perform the work the firms needs them do; staff careers are co-managed by the staff person and the firm's partners; marketing is done by partners; selling additional services to existing clients is made a priority; and an advertising program is developed and placed on schedule. Oversight or reporting methods are established and they are followed by all the partners and staff as necessary. Firm compliance issues need to be followed up on and client service kept to firm standards, as previously agreed to by the partners. Tax calendars are maintained and bottlenecks that develop need to be looked after regularly. The managing partner needs to be an enthusiastic cheer leader with proper vision and the mission to carry it out. The managing partner also needs to be the guardian of the firm culture.

Actually this is only the tip of the iceberg. The point I want to make is that running a firm takes serious effort and should not be relegated to moments you can steal from your "other" work. The problem is that most small firms don't take the managing partner job serious enough. Ditto for many larger firms with compensation models that discourage reduced chargeable time.

The really successful firms have full time dedicated managing partners *running the business.*

Larger firms can well afford this. I know many firms with less than 25 people that feel they cannot afford having their managing partner spend full time managing the firm. On some level they probably cannot afford having him or her spend part time either. The model in most CPA firms is to take the best rainmaker or the person handling the biggest client load (sometimes the same person) and make them the managing partner. It's done all the time, but it is a model that doesn't work. When that happens, I find that the firm stops growing. It may not shrink, but the growth stops. I can point to many dozen firms where this occurred and I am sure you can also think of many yourself. The model doesn't work, but everyone keeps doing it – to save the money needed to invest in growth.

A suggestion that doesn't change the model too much is for the managing partner to not think of themselves as the administrative partner and to hire a top flight assistant capable of performing all of the managing partner's administrative functions. In today's world this person would be called a chief operating officer. In earlier times it would be a firm administrator. This COO does not have to be a CPA and probably would be better if the person was a "professional" manager.

Cost justification is easy. A 10-person firm grosses around $2 million. Assume a COO would cost $100,000 (including taxes and benefits). That is 5% of volume, and a full $100,000 off of the net going to the partners. Presently you have your top rainmaker and client service partner reducing his/her workload to do the administrative functions. Let's say that person makes $250,000. This is like hiring another 40% of your best partner. If your "new" 40% managing partner cannot grow the firm enough to make back this $100,000, then you are off target and probably it doesn't matter what you do.

However, it is hard to believe the COO's costs wouldn't be covered and then some. Also the managing partner will be relieved of work that is below the best benefits he is capable of producing, the partner group will become better organized, more accountable and you will end up with better managed staff and a smoother functioning firm.

Ego justification is harder, but the managing partner would still run things, he just wouldn't be doing it on a day to day basis and would have a skilled assistant carrying on under him. Also with proper oversight and reporting he or she would have a complete handle on what is going on.

This model works for any size firm. The object is to have the partners do what each of them does best and not burden them with things they don't enjoy, do well or where they lack the skills and time and discipline to follow up and follow through with.

I am clear about this, and have seen it work. I also know that not doing this will stick the firm at its current level and wear down the better partners.

98. Effective Staffing

Q:

I have two people doing approximately the same work and need to let one go. The problem is one person is much better than the other, but she is a sourpuss.

Should I keep her, or stick with the nicer person?

A:

Take nice over smart. I want smart and nice people working for me. I don't want to have to choose between the two, but if I have to, I'll take nice every time, in every situation.

Get rid of aggravating people – Life's too short.

99. Complaining Client

Q:

I have had a client for 12 years and until recently he has been a pleasure.

For the last year he seems to be overly complaining about the fees and has fallen behind in payments. He is not hurting for cash so it is not a money issue.

What can I do to get the relationship back on track?

A:

I spoke at great length with the CPA and it seems that the client has been taken for granted and the accountant has dropped the ball.

Calls and emails were no longer returned quickly, an extension was filed this tax season for the first time in years, a long term staff person left so was replaced, and since client started to complain the partner hasn't been so anxious to interact with him. Also the CPA told me that the work has settled into a routine and nothing much has changed in years "so why should the client be upset now?"

The easiest and most non-confrontational thing a client can complain about is the fee. Some clients are natural and perpetual complainers, and we all know who they are. I am not talking about them and this client isn't one of them. When a client complains they do not want to end the relationship and are reaching out to you for help and to do something to make the problem go away or not reoccur. These have to be dealt with quickly.

Sometimes it's hard to recognize and needs you to be sensitive to signals and changes in patterns by the client. Also we sometimes forget with long standing clients that they know other accountants and are bombarded with requests to bid and take a look-see at what they are getting from existing accountants. When clients are taken for granted and no improvements in service or deliverables have been made in many years, doubt creeps into the client's minds that maybe things have changed and there is something better, or less expensive, especially when the client does not feel the "connection" anymore or has lost the feeling of a collaborative relationship with their accountant.

Things change. We have to be sensitive to this. There are many things we can do and should do. It is very important to not let client service get stale or blah.

When we get leads, we drop what we are doing to follow up and try to "Wow!" the prospect. I suggest we should be doing this continually with our existing clients. Don't they deserve it?

100. Thinking about Selling

Q:

I am getting ready to think about retiring. I don't want to work forever, and have enough saved so I will be pretty well off when I retire.

However, I would like to get the most that I could for my practice. I also would like my staff to not lose their jobs and for my clients to be well cared for. I am a sole practitioner with two part time bookkeepers, two full time CPAs and a full time secretary/office assistant. I have an informal relationship with a larger firm where I refer business I can't handle and they refer back smaller clients they do not want. They also do my peer review so are familiar with the quality of my work, which is pretty good. I met with the managing partner to see if they would be interested in acquiring my practice when I want to retire and they told me they weren't interested in smaller clients or 1040s, that I do not have a specialty they could capitalize on, and that my fee base is lower than their levels.

Whom do I go to?

A:

The most logical source is a firm about three times larger than you are so they could absorb your practice.

Anyone larger would probably have the same objections you've encountered, unless a larger firm wanted to open an office in your area, or you has a specialty they wanted to add to their practice, and then your size might not matter too much if they wanted to use your firm as a springboard to more business.

A smaller firm likely could not absorb your practice without special effort which many firms are not able to devote the right amount of time to. Some suggestions are to speak to firms in your area where you know a partner. This is possible when you attend society and chapter meetings and CPE and you spend time networking, and not on your smartphone during the breaks. Another thing that is very effective is signing up with a broker active in your area. Some of these are very effective. They also provide transition and making your practice more attractive advice. They advertise a lot, always write articles and give speeches, so they are easy to identify and approach. If you want a recommendation, give me a call.

A word about lower fee base: I haven't heard that as an objection to a merger or an acquisition.

It might be a factor in pricing the practice, but it is not a deal breaker. Every larger firm knows that smaller firms have either lower rates, provide extras they aren't compensated for, are subject to scope creep because of changing circumstances with the client, tax law changes or accounting pronouncements or simply neglect to increase fees for long periods of time.

They all feel that the fees can be increased *eventually* under their supposedly better service, procedures and systems. "Eventually" can be a number of years, but fees do increase.

I can tell you about our personal experience with buying a practice where the CPA's hourly rate was about 30% of ours and where everything he did was by the hour, and he did all the work at the clients' offices, never a minute in his office (except for typing financial statements).

Our rate at that time was $150 and his was $46. He was a sole practitioner and had three quality business clients that we felt would fit in well with our practice. He did not have that many 1040s and had a fourth business client that was more of a bookkeeping job that he wanted to keep.

Although he lived in Northern New Jersey two clients were near our East Brunswick office and one was in Manhattan where we also had an office. A perfect fit geographically.

This was in 1994. Everything he did was manual, he did not use any computers, including for tax returns. He typed his financial statements himself also charging $46 per hour.

When we agreed to buy his practice we had a schedule of the fees he collected during the past twelve months and we went to each client and told them nine things:

1. we would fix their fees at that amount for the next year and bill them monthly,

2. we would probably increase their fees a small percent each following year and not more;

3. they could terminate our services at any time for any reason;

4. any work that could be done at our office would be;

5. we would use staff people to perform many of the compliance services;

6. we would convert their bookkeeping to our computer systems at our expense;

7. if they wanted us to transfer to a computer on their premises we would, also at our expense;

8. a partner would be available to meet with them anytime they want for any reason; and

9. we would be fully accessible to them during normal business hours (this was before email and low cost cell phones).

For 1995, our first year, the average rate received was over $100 per hour. At the end of five years our fees were 50% higher (an average increase of less than 10% per year) with no dramatic jump in fees any one year.

We were putting in less time that we anticipated and the rates received were similar to our regular client base.

We also were able to bill for extra services that came up at fixed fees agreed to in advance where we averaged more per hour than our usual rates.

Further, our service was significantly better with quicker turnaround and more informative reports and financial data provided to the clients.

Coincidentally with buying this practice, my partner Frank started working for us and he worked on these three clients from the get go.

Since then, one went of business about five years ago, another is phasing down his business and the third has grown tremendously and is going strong with younger management.

Frank is the partner in charge of the two still in business. By the way, we did not do well with the 1040 retention.

The question of selling or merging always raises a lot of issues. I've organized some of the most important issues into a checklist...

32 Reasons To Do a Deal

1. Get greater volume

2. Make more money

3. The practice is available at an attractive price and terms

4. Get or attain a critical mass either in volume or a specialty

5. Acquire a specialty or expertise

6. Step into a reputation in a niche or service area

7. Better utilize partners in combined or larger firm

8. Have a spokesperson that is well known in the media

9. Operate in a geographic area or strategic location

10. Have better perception by clients of being a player in the marketplace

11. Get trained staff

12. Get needed management skills

13. Get needed administrative skills

14. Get clients in an industry

15. Step into valuable banking, bonding, legal or other relationships

16. Become a larger firm so that clients' increased needs for credit can be supported

17. Succession or transition planning reasons

18. Get young blood, or an elder statesman to accommodate client or referral base

19. Consolidate administrative, bookkeeping, technology and marketing functions to obtain better utilization at lower combined costs

20. Better access to technology, more sophisticated software, procedures and infrastructure

21. Freedom for most partners from admin and firm management

22. Partners not getting along personally

23. Partners who don't agree on the future direction of the firm

24. Partners who don't want to invest in the future

25. Move or obtain a new lease

26. Lost a tenant and need to fill space

27. Already have a good working relationship with merger partner

28. Business presently being referred elsewhere can be retained by the combined practice

29. Acquire a super rainmaker

30. A previously negotiated deal fell through and a need to act quickly

31. A death or disability and a practice continuation agreement is in effect

32. The smaller firm partners believe they can "take over" managing bigger firm

101. Future of Small CPA Firms

Q:

I have a small firm, just me and two part-time accountants and a secretary-receptionist-administrative assistant. I am 48 and have been in business 18 years and have never bought a practice or had a partner.

A lot of what you write about seems to pertain to larger practices.

I am concerned with the future of firms such as mine. I am always too busy working and the only time I get a new client seems to be when I lose one and I need to replace the revenue. Also, I started out primarily with write-ups and now everyone seems to be using QuickBooks® or similar software. Any ideas?

A:

Plenty!

For starters, I get a full range of calls from CPAs, some one-person shops working out of their houses with no staff. So you are not that small as far as my audience is concerned. Of course, some are much larger, but many of those started out working out of their house.

Now for some comments.

> 1. I suggest some soul searching to decide what you really want for the rest of your professional career. Do you want to grow your practice, grow professionally, make more money, work less, work

with a certain type of client or are you satisfied where you are?

2. If you are satisfied, then good for you and you don't have to do anything different

3. If not satisfied, you need to recognize that you are in a business and as such, need to run it like a business. Too many solo practitioners work as if they are CPAs pulling in a pay check. I suggest a mind-set change to becoming an entrepreneur. To help you, you need to read *The E-Myth Revisited* by Michael Gerber.

4. I believe there is a bright future for small CPA practices and firms. Most businesses are small and its owners prefer an accountant with expertise in their size company who is hands on, available and appears to be keeping slightly ahead of the curve. Size will not present you with a trophy; it's your touchy-feely qualities that will rule

5. Larger firms cannot have their partners devote too much time to any one client, with certain exceptions. The success of larger firms is tied into the partners' qualities and relationships with clients and the use of leverage so that staff can perform most of the services. Once there is staff, training, management and review procedures need to be in place so that the staff will do the right things, at the right times, the right way. This takes effort, resolve and a dedication to build a firm, not a larger practice

6. I think smaller firms are much better positioned to get new business. The decision makers are more accessible to the accountant and can make easier and quicker decisions. Everything is done one-on-one. The feedback I get is that good office positioning, belonging to organizations and advertising are all very effective in getting additional business

7. I know many small firms that make no effort to garner additional services and referrals from existing clients. This is low hanging fruit that is easy pickings – as long as you reach for it. I feel it is easier for smaller firms to get this extra business

8. Where smaller practices need help is with staffing and delegating. This takes effort and also learning how to do it and when enough is enough and when to back off. It also needs empowerment so that all decisions don't have to be made by the owner

9. I was in your position when clients started to need less work by me because they switched to QuickBooks. I learned QB, went with my staff to QB courses and became a QB consultant and business

advisor instead of an outsourced bookkeeper. Take a QB course and learn better how to use it.

10.　On some level tax preparation by CPAs is being abandoned to TurboTax® type of programs. We can still be tax planners and tax advisors, at higher rates, but at a reduced quantity of hours.

11. I believe smaller practices have great opportunities ahead but they need the desire, ability, and vision to seize their opportunities.

APPENDIX

Practice Continuation In Event Of A Death Or Disability

This memo has been prepared for illustration purposes and no opinions are made or intended. Further, to ensure compliance with U. S. Treasury rules, unless expressly stated otherwise, any U. S. tax advice contained in this communication (including attachments) is not intended or written to be used, and cannot be used, by the recipient for the purpose of avoiding penalties that may be imposed under the Internal Revenue Code.

The following sample agreement addresses a practices' transfer in event of a sole practitioner's or all of a firm's partners' sudden death; and the method of servicing clients in the event of a temporary or partial disability or inability to practice.

It is recommended that you execute a similar agreement with a fellow practitioner to protect your practice, clients and family wealth or cash flow.

The following was written in letter form without the guidance of an attorney. It would be advisable for you to have this arrangement reviewed by your attorney. Also, the tax treatment of the purchase and sale of Section 197 assets should be reviewed as of the date you execute such an agreement.

We suggest that you bring your spouse with you when you sign this agreement and explain to them the importance of quick action. An instructional letter is also illustrated.

Note that this letter represents the minimum that should be done and provides a method that can provide protection for the practice's value that can be quite effective under many circumstances.

Letter Agreement That Can Be Made With A Fellow Practitioner

Dear _____,

This letter is to give you our understanding of how we will acquire your practice.

In event of death

1. We will acquire your entire practice only in the event of your death during a time when there are no surviving partners of your practice. Upon your death, we will be contacted by   [spouse's name[or _____, either of whom will have the information necessary to effect the transfer of your practice and who are authorized to effect such transfer.

2. We will make a good-faith effort to retain the maximum number of your clients, but we will not be obligated to retain any clients we do not feel will be appropriate for our practice. We will make every effort to "sell" clients (on your behalf) that we don't wish to retain, but do not guarantee that we can or will sell such accounts. We will notify you as soon as we are sure we won't retain an account, but in no event later than six months after the files are turned over to us. In the event that we decide not to retain a client of yours, we will agree not to solicit or speak to that client for at least one (1) year following your death.

3. We will make a good-faith effort to sell those clients we decide not to retain, but we do not guarantee that we can or will sell such clients. If any of your clients that are not retained by us are sold through our efforts, we will pay to your estate eighty percent (80%) of the sales proceeds.

4. We will pay your estate (as used in this letter "your estate" will refer to either your, family or designated heirs, as the case may be and as indicated by you at the bottom of this letter) 20% of all fees billed and collected from your clients for all work done during the first five years of the transfer. This includes any work done for the client in every and all entities and business forms they operate or call themselves under and includes newly formed entities and ventures. It will not include fees from any referrals from those clients if the referring client has no financial or ownership interest in the new client.

5. We will use business efforts consistent with own practice regarding billing and collection for the work performed by us for your clients. We shall provide your estate or designated heirs periodic reports regarding the work performed for your clients by us and the billings and collections with respect to your clients retained by us. This information shall also be made available to them upon written request.

6. Please note that we are providing no client retention guarantees and that if a client is lost for any reason, your estate will not be entitled to any payments other than amounts based upon billings and collections by us.

7. We will make payments to your estate by the tenth (10) day of the month following the month we collect the fees. However, if we collect any sums from your clients on account of work performed by you prior to transfer (your accounts receivable), we will remit one-hundred percent (100%) of those amounts within ten (10) days of collection. Nothing herein shall constitute a sale, transfer or assignment of your accounts receivable to us.

8. Your estate will turn over your workpaper files and computer disks or backup and passwords for each client for the last three (3) years. We will assume all of your professional responsibilities for maintaining and retaining these files and disks. The files and disks will be made available to your estate upon written request as long as that request is consistent with our professional and ethical responsibilities. It will be our choice to keep or discard those files. However, if we decide to discard any of your files or disks during the period we are making payments to your estate or representatives, we must first notify your estate and will allow your estate to take back the files and disks.

9. We will also receive all office equipment used in your practice with the exception of personal items in your offices selected by your spouse, or children. We will pay rent on your office premises as long as we continue occupying the premises, but it is our intention to vacate the premises as soon as possible and we will not be responsible for the remaining portion of the lease. Any costs of vacating will be borne by us.

10. Upon our receipt of the files you will advise the telephone company to transfer the business telephone number to us; and you will give us ownership and access of any email addresses, websites, blog sites and social media names and addresses. We will also have the use of the deceased's name for two years following the transfer of the practice to us.

In event of temporary disability or inability to practice

11.   In the eventuality of a temporary disability or inability to practice we agree to service your clients until you recover and return to work. The determination of your ability to return to work is solely at your discretion.

12.   If you wish to return on a part time basis and want us to continue servicing selected clients, we will but we will solely perform the services on those clients without any client interaction by you.

13.   During the period that we service your clients, we will be paid 80% of the fees that are collected for the services we performed. If you return part time, we will be paid for the clients we work on, as if you have not returned, and will not have any of the fees prorated to take into account work you performed, if any.

14.   We will service your clients for a maximum period of one year. If you have not returned during that period, we will either be able to purchase the practice under the terms and conditions as if you died (see above), or terminate our services. We will not continue servicing your clients after one year of our commencement of services.

15.   After we stop servicing your clients in accordance with this agreement, and in the event that some of your clients wish us to continue as their accountants, we agree to pay you 150% of what we would have paid you had you died and we acquired this client for a period of five years, with the following exceptions: The five year payment will be based on billings and eventual collection during the first year and then that amount will become fixed and payable for the remaining four years regardless of whether the client is retained for that full period. If the client is not retained, the payments will be made monthly during the remaining period.

16.   During the period of disability or your inability to practice we will have access to the business telephone numbers, email addresses, websites, blog sites and social media names and addresses. If the transfer to us becomes permanent, then we will acquire ownership of them in accordance with the provision under the transfer because of death.

Tax treatment of payments

17.   With respect to death, all payments will be for the acquisition of the practice and will be treated as an installment sale of the practice with an

estimate made of the full payment based on 80% of the fees collected by the decedent during the last full calendar year preceding their death.

18. The buyer will treat the payments as payment for the acquisition of a Section 197 intangible asset and will amortize it over 15 years. The gross purchase price will be the amount calculated in accordance with the preceding paragraph.

19. At the earlier of the completion of five years after the sale, or when the aggregate payments exceed the initial purchase price, the buyer will include the extra payments as additional cost of the practice, and will add that amount to the unamortized purchase price and will amortize the new amount over the remaining period. The seller will treat the extra payments as capital gain in the tax year payments are received.

20. No interest will be included in any payments, nor will interest be imputed.

21. Both parties will prepare IRS Form 8594 and jointly agree to the amounts reflected on the form.

22. Payments with respect to disability or inability to practice will be treated as nonemployee compensation and deductible as such by the payer, and income by the disabled accountant.

General provisions

23. This agreement is not to be construed in any sense to constitute a partnership agreement between us, or between your estate and us.

24. This agreement will in no way confer any responsibility upon us for any work done before we took over.

25. This agreement is fully transferable by us should we merge or in any other way change our practice.

26. This agreement is not to be construed as a sale or transfer of your practice under any circumstances other than death or temporary disability or inability to practice as described above. Nothing herein shall prevent or prohibit you from retiring or selling your practice prior to your death or temporary disability or inability to practice, or making any other arrangements that you may wish. If you execute a similar agreement with someone else after

the date the agreement with us is signed, then this agreement will no longer be in effect.

27. This agreement is cancelable by either party at any time for any reason.

Designated heirs

For purposes of this agreement and payment, the designated heirs are
_____ and _____. Payments will be made to them equally.

If the above meets with your understanding, please sign a copy of this letter and return it to us. If you have any questions, please do not hesitate to call.

Cordially,

Instructional Letter To Accompany Practice Continuation Letter

Dear _____,

In connection with the agreement we signed today, following are some suggestions that could facilitate the transfer, should it become operative.

Nothing will be given to us unless the terms of the agreement are activated, and then the following should be provided as quickly as possible. Having this information available for your spouse or heirs to easily access is essential to a successful transfer or continuation of your practice as is a timely notification to us after the unfortunate event triggering the effectiveness of this agreement.

1. You should prepare a list of every client including the contact person, their telephone number and full type and frequency of service with the fees charged and other billing information.

2. It would be helpful to have your billing and collection information available for the previous year.

3. We need a list of passwords used by you in every case that they have been used including e-mail accounts.

4. The location of current and old files for your clients.

5. Any special client requests – such as the way, frequency, manner or form they want information; whether they only want e-mails, or no faxes, or visa versa; whether they hate extensions or only want extensions; financial planning or estate, succession or retirement planning desires; family issues; or anything else that will help us retain and better serve the client.

6. A schedule of fees due you either billed or unbilled, and work in progress, or where these are maintained in your accounting system or records

7. Since timeliness is of the essence, it would be necessary for us to contact each client as soon as possible. We should meet with your wife, or family, and discuss how this procedure will occur, but if it appears that will cause a delay in our calls, we will proceed as quickly as we feel necessary.

8. It is important for your spouse and/or family to be aware of this arrangement and to understand the importance of it to them and how it will work. You should discuss it with them, and if you wish, we would like to be present when this is done.

If you have any questions or comments, please do not hesitate to call.

Cordially,

Afterword

Email or call me with your practice management questions, or any comments about this book. Also, email me to be placed on my list for the monthly Q&As as posted and practice management checklists as issued. Also, sign up for my twice a week Blog that deals with issues my clients are concerned with.

Email: emendlowitz@withum. com

Tel 732 964-9329

Blog: www. partners-network. com

– Ed Mendlowitz

More by Ed Mendlowitz from CPA Trendlines

At cpaclick. com/shopcpa

Tax Season Opportunity Guide

How to Increase Your Billing Rates

The 30:30 Training Method

How to Review Tax Returns

More from CPA Trendlines

At cpaclick. com/shopcpa

Professional Services Marketing 3. 0, by Bruce W. Marcus

How To Bring in New Partners

Rosenberg MAP Survey

How to Negotiate a CPA Firm Merger

CPA Firm Succession Planning: A Perfect Storm

CPA Firm Management & Governance

Creating The Effective Partnership: Two-Volume Package

- Leadership At Its Strongest
- How to Engage Partners in the Firm's Future

The Client Service Idea Book

Accounting Marketing 101 for Partners

How CPA Firms Work: The Business of Public Accounting

The Accountant's (Bad) Joke Book

Strategic Planning and Goal Setting for Results

What Really Makes CPA Firms Profitable?

How to Operate a Compensation Committee

Guide to Planning the Firm Retreat

Effective Partner Relations and Communications

The Idea Book for Accounting Firm Hiring Managers:

The Idea Book for Career Planning in Accounting

Survey Report: Busy Season Barometer of Operating Results

Survey Report: Marketing and Business Development Trends

CPA Trendlines provides actionable intelligence and practical guidance to tax, accounting and finance professionals and the vendors who serve them. The website cpatrendlines. com is updated daily and available in its entirety to Pro Members. Join at GoProCPA. com

Made in the USA
Charleston, SC
28 July 2014